Turn Into the Wind

Turn Into the Wind

Prayers and Reflections

by College Students

Edited by Shirley Kelter

Saint Mary's Press
Christian Brothers Publications
Winona, Minnesota

Genuine recycled paper with 10% post-consumer waste.
Printed with soy-based ink.

The publishing team included Shirley Kelter, develop-
ment editor; Laurie A. Berg, copy editor; James H.
Gurley, production editor and typesetter; Maurine R.
Twait, art director; Cindi Ramm, graphic designer;
Vernon Sigl, cover photo; pre-press, printing, and
binding by the graphics division of Saint Mary's
Press.

The acknowledgments continue on page 151.

Printed in the United States of America

Printing: 9 8 7 6 5 4 3 2 1

Year: 2007 06 05 04 03 02 01 00 99

ISBN 0-88489-575-0

PREFACE

In the fall of 1997, Saint Mary's Press invited students from colleges and universities throughout the United States to submit prayers, poems, or reflections on their favorite Scripture passages for this publication. Students responded enthusiastically, and several professors sent in bundles of reflections, products of a class assignment. From the many submissions, these one hundred seventeen were selected because they expressed a variety of ideas, emotions, spiritualities, and issues relevant to young adults.

For over fifty years, it has been the mission of Saint Mary's Press to bring the good news to young people and, whenever possible, to draw on the gifts of our audience, especially the young writers and artists. We are grateful to all the students who participated in this project and to the many instructors, campus ministers, and chaplains who supported our effort.

Courage, Surrender, Spirit

Turn Into the Wind is filled with stories of courage. The prayers, poems, and reflections offered in this book address the issues and concerns flying at college students—sometimes like a gentle wind, sometimes like a hurricane: pressures, expectations, passions, fears, doubts, complicated relationships, newfound independence, hopes, and dreams. A recurring message that I hear from the student writers is this: Don't run away or shrink from these issues. Rather, have courage and turn into them—face them head-on.

Turn Into the Wind is filled with stories of vulnerability and surrender. One student wrote, "It's hard to be chosen . . . to turn into the wind that blows my mask away." To be "mask-less" is to be vulnerable. It takes great courage to surrender our masks, to expose our real selves. College is an ideal time to take such a risk, to try on our real selves, to be true to ourselves and others. This is what growing in integrity is all about.

Turn Into the Wind is filled with stories of God. The Hebrew term for spirit is *ruah,* meaning "wind," understood sometimes as the breath of Yahweh—the life-giving element. Each writer in this book has shared part of his or her soul—the very breath of God swirling or rushing within. Readers are invited to turn toward God, who dwells in their own sacred space.

Entering Prayer

This book seeks to engage you in dialog with God. Following are a few ideas for using the book that might enrich your prayer experience.

Savor the Word of God

Don't rush through this book, but try to take it a page at a time, maybe a page each day. Find a chunk of uninterrupted quiet time for yourself, and begin by closing your eyes and simply breathing deeply, letting go of any tension or anxiety you might be feeling. Let yourself be aware of God's presence, and rest comfortably in that peace and stillness. Come to your prayer with an open mind, heart, and will.

When you feel calm and centered, read the Scripture passage on the page you've chosen. Read it slowly, say it aloud if you can, linger on the words, and let them seep into you. Perhaps a word or phrase jumps out at you; sit with it for a minute or two and let it reach into you. Is a question being asked in the quote? Read it as though it were addressed to you. How would you answer? Remember, the Bible is not simply a history book but the living word of God. It is meant for us, today.

If you enjoy writing, you may wish to keep a journal of your reflections or to write directly on the page you're reading. Underline or highlight the words that are meaningful, and add your own. Jot down a feeling you have as you read the Scripture passage, or a question that surfaces. Write the name of a person the passage brings to mind, or someone who is especially in need of prayer today.

CONSIDER THE REFLECTION OFFERED

Other college students have spent time with these same Scripture verses, and they share their reflections with you in this book. Their thoughts might be quite different from yours, and you could gain a new insight through their words. Explore how the truths they express speak to your truth—your experiences, questions, and beliefs.

Gather Two or More

Consider gathering a group of friends for faith sharing, using this book as a tool. Begin with quiet time for centering. Have one person read the selected passage aloud, then spend a few more minutes in silence for personal reflection. Those who wish to can share their thoughts with the group and discuss implications of the passage. Then read the writer's reflection, and continue the discussion. Perhaps the group will want to take some action in response to what they have shared. For example, each person might agree to read that passage daily until the next time the group meets. Or each person may decide to write a note or letter to someone who could benefit from receiving this passage. A group might commit to some expression of justice in response to a passage that challenges them to live authentically the Gospels.

At the end of the discussion, the group could offer prayers of petition and thanksgiving, say the Lord's Prayer together, and share a sign of peace with one another.

Community enriches prayer. Find ways to pray together that help you grow as soul-companions.

Blessings

As the editor of this book, it has been a privilege to be invited into the depths of these students' spirits where God dwells, swept up in the wind that is God's spirit and that reaches into my own soul.

As you encounter God in this book, may you gain clear insights, bold vision, fresh hope, and a renewed faith from the reflections and stories offered by your peers. Blessings upon each of you as you journey through these rich and adventure-filled years of college.

Shirley Kelter
Editor

Reflections

WE KNOW *that all things work together for good for those who love God, who are called according to his purpose.*

(Romans 8:28)

Oh, how the days passed—
Here I lived without really being aware.
So many sunrises and sunsets gone by and
My life remained harmonious and undisturbed.
Unknowingly, I forgot to thank God for all
those perfect days—
The mornings that flowed smoothly into night,
And the nights that invited a peaceful slumber.
But now I am faced with hardships—
Every morning has turned into an obstacle,
And the quiet sleep is all but absent.
It would be easy to cry to God, "Why me?"
But would God not think me foolish?
For when that good fortune slipped by,
Not once did I ask, "Why me?"
Whether our lives be full of splendor or tragedy,
God forever reminds us that
Everything happens for a reason.
As long as we live in the light of God,
And thank God for all our days,
Unending love and comfort is ours.
All God asks is that we trust.

Christine Melko
Viterbo College
La Crosse, Wisconsin

TRUST IN THE LORD *with all your heart,*
and do not rely on your own insight.
In all your ways acknowledge him,
and he will make straight your paths.

(Proverbs 3:5–6)

Many of us are rapidly approaching gradua-
tion, and I am often struck by feelings of both
excitement and apprehension: excitement
about change and the vast opportunities that
lie ahead, and apprehension about the many
choices that will inevitably have to be made.

This verse from Proverbs is so encouraging! I
find it to be the epitome of faith that God calls
us to. How easy it can be for us to read past
such promises without stopping to take them to
heart. I'm not advocating that we take these
verses to an extreme and not apply for a job or
further schooling—that would be ridiculous.
However, we can reflect on these words and
hide them in our heart, letting God's word be a
constant source of strength when we are faced
with times of uncertainty and anxiety.

Jennifer Elam
Saint Mary's University of Minnesota
Winona, Minnesota

COME TO ME, *all you that are weary and are carrying heavy burdens, and I will give you rest.*
(Matthew 11:28)

Oh, God! I come to you with a heavy, weary heart and mind. I am so busy at school—with classes, meetings, exams, papers . . . I could go on! Even when I go to Mass, I cannot shut my brain off. I constantly have things running through my head: I forgot to call this person back, set up this meeting, finish that paper.

God, grant me a sense of peace. Allow me to shove aside all those concerns that crowd my heart and keep me from opening the door to you. Enter into my heart and mind and surround me with stillness. Grant my whole being a sense of calm so I can be more focused on you. Then I can stop worrying and realize that all I need in my life is you.

Molly Buettner
University of Scranton
Scranton, Pennsylvania

†AKE CARE! *Be on your guard against all kinds of greed; for one's life does not consist in the abundance of possessions.*

(Luke 12:15)

We college students always have so much on our mind. We worry about papers, tests, deadlines, school events, friends, and money. During my five years of college, I have had many jobs to support myself. Between the stresses of studying and making enough money to eat my next meal, I have often wished that I had a full-time job and was done with college.

Now as I am finishing my senior year, I am still broke, I will be in debt for years to come, and I drive a car that is older than I am—but something else is different. I'm happy for who I am and what I have done. I've had so many great experiences over the last five years that I would not trade for any amount of money. I met a lot of people, had great times, and, most important, I learned who I am and what I want out of life. This is what college is really about— learning for tomorrow and living for today!

Krista Kathryn Webb
Viterbo College
La Crosse, Wisconsin

JESUS SAID TO THEM, *"I am the bread of life. Whoever comes to me will never be hungry, and whoever believes in me will never be thirsty. But I said to you that you have seen me and yet do not believe. Everything that the Father gives me will come to me, and anyone who comes to me I will never drive away; for I have come down from heaven, not to do my own will, but the will of him who sent me.*

(John 6:35–38)

The key weighs heavy in my hand.
I have not opened this door since happier days.
Seeing the familiar cracked frame and scars in
the wood carries me back.
What I have been searching for
is behind this gateway.
I have left it hidden, . . .
Allowing myself to destroy and be destroyed,
Finding all other ways to fill the hole.
That is why I am here;
There is nothing more of me.
Calling calling . . .
His voice is a constant echo in my ears.
Come to me,
But I resist,
Knowing I will have to give myself,
But I am lost.
So I offer myself up.
The key clicks in the keyhole,
and the door swings open.

The Lord is there, where he has always been,
Waiting for me.
I am home.

Lisa Marie Rose Brandt
Saint Mary's University of Minnesota
Winona, Minnesota

EVERY DAY, *as long as this today lasts, keep encouraging one another so that none of you is hardened by the lure of sin.*

(Hebrews 3:13, NJB)

College is a time of rapid growth and change. From the time we first arrive on campus until the time we leave, we are confronted by opportunities, and sometimes demands, for change.

But not all change is good, not all opportunities should be welcomed, and not every demand should gain our assent. As Christians we live *in* the world but are not *of* the world. We are called to struggle daily in our efforts to live out our faith.

Amid this struggle is the temptation to sin. Sex outside of marriage, drug and alcohol abuse, and cheating to pass a course are not the only ways we can betray our faith on campus. Anger, gossip, envy, uncharitable behavior toward faculty and fellow students, and skipping Sunday Mass are far more common sins that harden our heart and turn us away from God.

Standing alone against these temptations only invites failure. We must join together in prayer, and daily encourage one another to lead faithful lives while it is still today.

Will Ferguson
Saint Vincent College
Latrobe, Pennsylvania

THEN THE LORD GOD *formed man*
from the dust of the ground, and breathed into his
nostrils the breath of life; and the man became a
living being.

(Genesis 2:7)

Lord, look on me with tenderness.
Have mercy on me.
Be my shade and my sun,
my solace and my smile
as I strive to surrender myself to you,
making my soul supple to your spirit,
to your hands which continually create me.
I try to cooperate with you,
accepting myself as I am now
and looking forward to the person
whom I have yet to become.
As you provide opportunities for me to grow,
I reconcile myself with the uncertainty
that comes with change,
and I concentrate on birthing myself
into a new maturity,
a new and better "me,"
which is the reward of my struggles.
I pray that I may always invest
complete trust in you,
knowing that with your gentle hands
molding me and providing direction for my life,
I have nothing to fear.
I know that the potholes of the soul
are bound to surface
when I least expect them to—
times when my weaknesses
manifest themselves

through my human stumblings—
but with you, dear God, by my side,
insulating me with your peace,
I have the hope
that I will not grow discouraged,
but will only be inspired to serve you
with my whole heart and my whole soul,
more and more every day,
until my days become one
in eternity
through your gift of salvation.
Amen.

Jennifer Dudeck
Douglass College, Rutgers University
New Brunswick, New Jersey

JUST AS YOU DID IT *to one of the least of these who are members of my family, you did it to me.*

(Matthew 25:40)

Last summer I had the opportunity to volunteer in Santa Catarina, Mexico, for seven weeks. There a team of seven other students and a priest lived and worked at a home for poor young boys who came from broken homes, other orphanages, or the street. Their hearts cried out for many things, even though their physical needs were now being satisfied. We didn't come to build them a school or to teach them English. We came to be friends and role models. The bonds we formed cannot be broken by distance—we shared in their meals, sports, games, studies, and their Eucharist. We climbed volcanoes, played cards, took walks, had long conversations with them. We did all of this in Christ's name. I have never so fully believed that I had looked Christ in the eye, shared a laugh with him, wiped a tear off his face, and embraced him in friendship and love.

We truly are all one body in Christ.

Molly Buettner
University of Scranton
Scranton, Pennsylvania

CAST ALL YOUR ANXIETY *on him,*
because he cares for you.

(1 Peter 5:7)

There's only one who knows . . .
    how I truly feel,
    if I'm happy or sad;
  One who understands
    that I can be both at the same time.
There's only one who really knows . . .
    my pains and fears;
  One who can comfort both in a special way.
There's only one who knows . . .
    all the things that happen to me
    and all that I feel;
  One that makes me all that I am.
There's only one who knows . . .
    that sometimes I doubt his presence
    and feel all alone;
  One who is always with me.
There's only one who knows . . .
    that I do not need to try all kinds of tricks,
    knock and knock,
    or even yell to get his attention;
  One who will come . . . if only I ask.

Malinda Kesteloot
University of Northern Iowa
Fort Dodge, Iowa

AS GOD'S CHOSEN ONES, *holy and beloved, clothe yourselves with compassion, kindness, humility, meekness, and patience. Bear with one another and, if anyone has a complaint against another, forgive each other; just as the Lord has forgiven you, so you also must forgive. Above all, clothe yourselves with love, which binds everything together in perfect harmony.*

(Colossians 3:12–14)

We face difficult decisions every day. How we react to those difficult situations determines who we are as human beings: we can simply follow the law and customs of our culture, or we can live above and beyond these acceptable norms.

Saint Paul clearly tells us what is expected of us as Christian people: we are called to compassion, kindness, humility, meekness, and patience. Incorporating these virtues into our life is hardly an easy task. Perhaps that is why Saint Paul chooses to include the notion of forgiveness. Forgiveness is not a gift that is always given freely and easily, but it is necessary if we are to attempt to live a Christian life.

Saint Paul offers the purest way to leading a Christian life— "Clothe yourselves with love, which binds everything together in perfect harmony." We are not perfect, but we can have hope that by incorporating love into our life, we can grow closer to being the person—and community—that God has called us to be.

Jill Arens
Saint Mary's University of Minnesota
Winona, Minnesota

THEREFORE, *since we are surrounded by so great a cloud of witnesses, let us also lay aside every weight and the sin that clings so closely, and let us run with perseverance the race that is set before us.*

(Hebrews 12:1)

Recently I found myself in the midst of a difficult crisis. A friend suggested that I read about Hannah in the First Book of Samuel, and I took great comfort from her story. I also remembered other stories of people who had cried out to a faithful God in the midst of personal suffering. Some were biblical stories, others were written memoirs of famous Christians past and present, and still others were stories told to me by friends.

This brought to mind the "great . . . cloud of witnesses" from Hebrews. My cloud of witnesses includes those people whose stories I store up in my heart and take comfort from in times of distress. My faith, my ability to "run with perseverance the race that is set before" me, is intricately tied up in this community of faith. During my recent crisis, the cloud of witnesses became very real to me. At the same time that I felt deep emotional pain, God gave me a strong sense of all those who had gone before—walking with me, passing me gently from one to the other, seeing me safely to my destination of healing.

Susan E. McNitt
Boston University
Boston, Massachusetts

MY GOD, MY GOD, *why have you
forsaken me?*
*Why are you so far from helping me, from the
words of my groaning? . . .*
But you, O LORD, do not be far away! . . .
*Future generations will . . . proclaim his
deliverance to a people yet unborn,
saying that he has done it.*

(Psalm 22:1,19,30–31)

My God, my God, why have I forsaken you?
  Why am I so far from your ways?
Oh, my God, I know your love
  and your magnificence.
Day and night I cry out,
  not to you, O God,
  but to the still of the earth.
In times of deepest despair I sink,
  then my eyes are drawn to the light.
You were here, right here with me,
  even when I placed you second in my longing.
I have trusted you all my life.
I praise your name in hopes of the future,
  that I may call on you in the very moment
  of sorrow or joy.
For it is you who lives within me,
  strengthening me.
You will provide,
  for you have done it.

Michelle Yvette Bissman
Lycoming College
Williamsport, Pennsylvania

JESUS ALSO SUFFERED *outside the city gate in order to sanctify the people by his own blood. Let us then go to him outside the camp and bear the abuse he endured.*

(Hebrews 13:12–13)

A year ago I stood in the crowded Philadelphia airport clutching my sister's hands so tightly that sweat rolled off onto the sleeves of my winter jacket. The world felt moist as my eyes released heavy, warm tears onto my cheeks. It hurt. My vision blurred the signs marked Gate E4 and Now Boarding as the figures of my parents and my brother drifted farther away from me. They disappeared beyond the gate that led to the plane, leaving my sister and me behind, desperately alone.

I have wept days and nights for my loss. But it's about more than saying good-bye to my parents as they returned to West Africa. It's about losing a piece of myself as well. I have no family to share my dreams with. I have no one to cry to. I have no home. I stand with my feet planted in the soft earth beneath me, pausing in my journey up the hill of life. I turn to see my past lying beneath me: my childhood in Nigeria, my deep love for my family, the inevitability of coming to the United States for college and leaving home behind. Suddenly, without my family by my side, I feel the sting of loneliness. But I know they feel it, too. Momma often writes to me about how she cries over this painful separation from her children.

Oceans lie between us. I turn once more to look at the large hill that stands in my path, and I remember that God tells us that we need to make sacrifices when we serve. Jesus carried his heavy cross outside the city gates to where burnt offerings were made. Why do people suffer? If we follow Jesus, sacrifice is inescapable. And sometimes that sacrifice is our own family.

Martha Claire Truxton
Messiah College
Grantham, Pennsylvania

IF YOU BELONGED *to the world, the world would love you as its own. . . . You do not belong to the world, but I have chosen you out of the world.*

(John 15:19)

it's hard to be the one chosen
    to believe in the dawn that follows the
       darkest of nights
    to trust in the flame of a single candle
       knowing that even the tiniest of lights
       eliminates my only hiding place
    to follow this pathway to the bend in the road
       and beyond
    to turn into the wind that blows my mask away
       leaving me vulnerable for all the world to see
    to speak when no one is listening
    to listen when the world is silent
    to sing out, even without accompaniment
    to rest in the "I love you anyway, no matter what"
    to let go and be touched, stretched, molded
    to risk laughter, to tempt solitude
    to say *yes* with lips of praise and questions
    to mean *yes* with a mind of strength and
       patience
    to believe *yes* with a heart of love and pieces
       waiting
    to live *yes* with hands of faith and grace
yes, God, it's hard to be the one chosen
make me yours

j. a. g.
Duke University
Durham, North Carolina

FOR SURELY I KNOW *the plans I have for you, says the* LORD, *plans for your welfare and not for harm, to give you a future with hope. Then when you call upon me and come and pray to me, I will hear you.*

(Jeremiah 29:11–12)

I used to pencil prayer into my daily planner as if God were another Ph.D. I studied theology and volunteered in my free time, yet I still felt empty inside. In my hurried schedule, I was reaching out to others without taking the time to face the brokenness within me. I realized that I had to confront myself, let go of control of my own life, and, amid joy and struggles, trust in God's plan—not easy for a "type-A" personality. I began to reflect on the Scriptures each morning, and over time I came to understand myself, know Jesus better, and recognize the Holy Spirit working in my life. By making daily plans with God and learning to trust in God's plan for me, I found inner peace.

Gretchen M. Baumgardt
Saint Mary's University of Minnesota
Winona, Minnesota

COME TO ME, *all you that are weary and are carrying heavy burdens, and I will give you rest. Take my yoke upon you, and learn from me; for I am gentle and humble in heart, and you will find rest for your souls. For my yoke is easy, and my burden is light.*

(Matthew 11:28–30)

Leaves

Yesterday's secrets
lie scattered and torn like so
many fallen leaves.
Let them go into the wind,
or gather them for a fire.

Michael R. Guerin
Saint John's University
Jamaica, New York

TRUST IN THE LORD *with all your heart, and do not rely on your own insight. In all your ways acknowledge him, and he will make straight your paths."*

This day, away from home and in a new place,
remind me, dear God, that you are by my side.
Help me to trust in you fully
and to follow your word unquestionably
as I walk down the path that you have chosen
  for me.
May I always know that I need not fear
  slipping or falling,
for, if I have faith in you, you will catch me
and set me on my feet again.
In times of peace as well as in times of sorrow,
may I remember that you are always guiding
  me;
you are my shepherd, my God. Amen.

Jaimie D. Okusko
Viterbo College
La Crosse, Wisconsin

FOR GOD ALONE *my soul waits in silence,*
  for my hope is from him.
He alone is my rock and my salvation,
  my fortress; I shall not be shaken.
On God rests my deliverance and my honor;
  my mighty rock, my refuge is in God.
Trust in him at all times, O people;
  pour out your heart before him;
  God is a refuge for us.

(Psalm 62:5–8)

I am exhausted, but I can't rest. I can't sleep. I can't even sit still. My mind is dashing in half-a-gazillion directions. Rest eludes me.

Life is so full of junk that sorting through all of it is just too much, making me tired, weary, insecure, and empty. I can't find what I'm looking for by looking for it. God is what I need and what I desire: hope, salvation, a fortress, honor, a refuge. God taps me on the shoulder. But I can't see because I'm staring at the garbage pile of life and asking, "Why, God?"

Yet, the command is to rest, to be quiet, to sit still, to know beyond all shadow of a doubt that God is in complete control. And to know that in all times, all places, and for all peoples, God is good. Rest alludes to the presence of the Savior.

Missy Graham
Wesleyan College
Macon, Georgia

THE LORD *is my shepherd, I shall not want.*
  He makes me lie down in green pastures;
he leads me beside still waters;
  he restores my soul.
He leads me in right paths
  for his name's sake.
Even though I walk through the darkest valley,
  I fear no evil;
for you are with me;
  your rod and your staff—
  they comfort me.

(Psalm 23:1–4)

Dear Lord, I come in prayer once again,
asking you to watch over and
guide my grandmother;
she is quite ill, so I must leave her
in your hands.
Let the outcome be your omnipotent will.
Love surrounds her here on earth,
as she has surrounded us with
her undying devotion.
She always had time, love, and patience for me;
now I must stand beside her in this
treacherous time.
She is loved dearly;
however, if she is done with her time here,
take her softly and quickly home.
Amen.

Elzie Burgher
Saint Catharine College
Saint Catharine, Kentucky

BLESSED *be the Lord,*
  for he has heard the sound of my pleadings.
The Lord is my strength and my shield;
  in him my heart trusts;
so I am helped, and my heart exults,
  and with my song I give thanks to him.

(Psalm 28:6–7)

Thank you, God, for being by my side in
troubled times,
For being a friend when I did not have one.
Thank you, God, for giving me a shoulder to
cry on when I had none.
Thank you for staying by my side when I
walked through foreign lands,
For always giving me a guiding hand
when one was needed.
Even when I have turned away from you, God,
you still stood by me.
You helped me understand others and myself.
Even though I have strayed in the past,
I will always try to walk in your light,
and with your guidance.
Amen.

Amie L. Patterson
Fort Lewis College
Durango, Colorado

AND IF I HAVE *prophetic powers, and understand all mysteries and all knowledge, and if I have all faith, so as to remove mountains, but do not have love, I am nothing. If I give away all my possessions, and if I hand over my body so that I may boast, but do not have love, I gain nothing.*
(1 Corinthians 13:2–3)

As I write this, I have barely enough money in my pocket to do the overflowing load of laundry piled in the corner of my dorm room. As a student of social work who is going to enter the seminary after I graduate, I have accepted that I will probably never be wealthy in material items or capital gains. I don't own a car or a computer. I don't have a stereo, and my sneakers are wearing a little thin on the sides and bottom—but you know what? I am still very happy. Jesus loves me, and I love him. I have a family who loves me, and I love them. I have friends who love me, and I love them. LOVE. Isn't that enough? After all, if we don't have love, we don't have anything.

Paul Wayne Benjamin
SUNY College at New Paltz
New Paltz, New York

ꟿY CHILD, *if you accept my words*
and treasure up my commandments within you,
making your ear attentive to wisdom
and inclining your heart to understanding;
if you indeed cry out for insight,
and raise your voice for understanding;
if you seek it like silver,
and search for it as for hidden treasures—
then you will understand the fear of the LORD
and find the knowledge of God.

(Proverbs 2:1–5)

Lord, from you comes knowledge,
understanding, and justice.
You are the guardian of us all, watching over us
and maintaining the path of the faithful.
I embrace your words and cherish your laws.
Compel my ears to be vigilant to hearing wisdom,
and evoke my heart to understanding your truth.
I seek to know you, Lord.
I yearn for insight and cry out for understanding.
Teach me your ways so that wisdom may enter
my heart and my soul.
Teach me your ways so that evil cannot steer
me away from you.
Be with me as I venture on the way
of the good and faithful.
Guide me as I walk the path of the just.
Give me grace to live my life
So that I may see your face
at the end of my days, O Lord.

Karin McConville
Saint Mary's University of Minnesota
Winona, Minnesota

†HEN HE WiTHDREW *from them about a stone's throw, knelt down, and prayed, "Father, if you are willing, remove this cup from me; yet, not my will but yours be done." Then an angel from heaven appeared to him and gave him strength. In his anguish he prayed more earnestly, and his sweat became like great drops of blood falling down on the ground.*

(Luke 22:41–44)

Almighty God, even as you strengthened your Son in his hour of darkness, you are my strength in time of need. When all seems lost and I feel alone, confused, or frightened, let me not forget that you are always with me, that your love is steadfast, and that nothing can overcome the power of that love. O God, send quickly your Spirit, the Comforter, that I may rejoice in hope—the hope that only you can give. I ask this through our Lord Jesus Christ, who lives and reigns with you in the unity of the Holy Spirit, one God, now and forever. Amen.

Scott W. Hoffman
Purdue University
West Lafayette, Indiana

MY BROTHERS AND SISTERS, *whenever
you face trials of any kind, consider it nothing but
joy, because you know that the testing of your faith
produces endurance; and let endurance have its full
effect, so that you may be mature and complete,
lacking in nothing.*

(James 1:2–4)

Sweet Jesus, take my hand
When another mountain looms ahead,
For I cannot climb alone.
Though the ground may start quaking
And my faith be shaken,
I'll hold on tightly to you.
When at last we reach the top
and look over the valley of my trial,
I'll weep in joy with you.
Sweet Jesus, in your peaceful embrace
I have the courage to face another mountain,
For you are my strength and my guide.

Gretchen M. Baumgardt
Saint Mary's University of Minnesota
Winona, Minnesota

"ASK, *and it will be given you; search, and you will find; knock, and the door will be opened for you. For everyone who asks receives, and everyone who searches finds, and for everyone who knocks, the door will be opened.*"

(Matthew 7:7–8)

Often I grow frustrated and discouraged that I am just not growing any closer to God. Despite my efforts I don't feel I'm making much progress toward where I would like to be spiritually. It is when I struggle that these verses from Matthew comfort me most. God has promised to give us whatever we ask for; certainly, then, we will be strengthened in our spiritual journey. When I try on my own to get closer to God, I inevitably fail. But when I ask God to draw me closer—God always answers.

K. G.
Saint Mary's University of Minnesota
Winona, Minnesota

"COME TO ME, *all you that are weary . . .
and I will give you rest. Take my yoke upon you,
and learn from me; for I am gentle and humble in
heart, and you will find rest for your souls. For my
yoke is easy, and my burden is light."*

(Matthew 11:28–30)

He was the only One
In my world at that moment
When life's burdens threatened to buckle me,
Leave me lying by the side of the road,
A regrettable casualty of the negative
Vicissitudes of this sojourn on Earth.

He silently called me to gaze at him.
Love, compassion, and understanding
His only expressions,
He said, "Do not fear."
I told him the truth, that I was wandering,
That my soul cried for understanding.
I knew then that he was that other,
And that later he would give me my soul mate.
"You have me always with you," he said.
"In me you have rest and comfort.
Come to me, and I will love you and keep you
    safe."
He touched my face; his strength poured into me.
He led me to peace after the storm.
I love you.

Elizabeth Lauren Costello
Connecticut College
New London, Connecticut

LOVE IS PATIENT; *love is kind; love is not envious or boastful or arrogant or rude. It does not insist on its own way; it is not irritable or resentful; it does not rejoice in wrongdoing, but rejoices in the truth. It bears all things, believes all things, hopes all things, endures all things.*

(1 Corinthians 13:4–7)

Gracious heavenly Lord, your hands extend toward me from as far as the east is from the west, embracing me. Provide me with strength and courage to stretch out my own hands to a society that has virtually turned its back on you, our Creator. Allow me the strength to love in such an evil world, and not to be rude or selfish. Help me bring compassion and happiness that will lead others to you. Then, Lord, give me patience and determination so I will not be discouraged on my own journey. Because we are a flawed humanity, this world desperately needs your unconditional love. Amen.

Tricia
Saint Catharine College
Saint Catharine, Kentucky

"ASK, *and it will be given you; search, and you will find; knock, and the door will be opened for you.*"

(Matthew 7:7)

There are times when I look and cannot find
When all the world's worries
   come down on my mind
When I stumble and fall
   along life's path as it winds.
Then I finally notice,
You're only one step behind.

Kelly Anne Dobson
Saint John's University
Jamaica, New York

"BLESSED *are the meek, for they will inherit the earth.*

"Blessed are those who hunger and thirst for righteousness, for they will be filled.

"Blessed are the merciful, for they will receive mercy.

"Blessed are the pure in heart, for they will see God."

(Matthew 5:5–8)

You Changed Mine

—A reflection at El Casita, a community soup kitchen near Duran, Ecuador

I came here because of a calling
   a calling to serve you
   a calling to help you
   a calling to know you
   a calling to be with you.

Completely knowing your life was different than mine
Completely intending to change your life

You smiled effortlessly and tugged my pant leg
as I walked off the bus,
encouraging me to feel your love
and the way you honored life.
I just smiled and felt awe
as I replayed those moments in my mind
when I first saw you
   your conditions
   your environment
and wondered
   how survival was possible

how life was possible
how love was possible.

But when I looked up and wiped the sweat from
my brow,
I felt your most trusting grasp on my hand.

Simple and with no hesitation
  you've shown me life
  you've shown me love
  you've shown me God
you've shown me more than I could ever
imagine.

I came here because of a calling.
  Instead, you called me.
A calling to serve you.
  Instead, you served me.
A calling to help you.
  Instead, you helped me.
A calling to know you.
  Instead, you challenged me.
A calling to be with you.
  Instead, you became a part of me.

Completely knowing your life was different
than mine
Completely intending to change your life

You changed mine.

Christopher N. Steel
University of Scranton
Scranton, Pennsylvania

MY BROTHERS AND SISTERS, *whenever you face trials of any kind, consider it nothing but joy, because you know that the testing of your faith produces endurance; and let endurance have its full effect, so that you may be mature and complete, lacking in nothing.*

(James 1:2–4)

Loving God,
Sometimes it seems that my problems are small compared to the problems of others I know. People say, though, that I have survived a lot of problems; often they ask me why I am so strong. God, the answer is simple! The answer is *you*. You promised that I will never have a problem that you and I can't conquer together. Knowing that you are on my side, I can deal with anything.

I thank you, God, for all the lessons that I have learned from my problems—especially for the patience you teach me. When I feel like a problem is more than I can handle, that it might destroy me, you come through with a lesson to be learned and a solution to be found in it. Thank you, God, for showing me that you will make all things possible. Amen.

Amanda Newman
Luther College
Decorah, Iowa

HE SAID *to him, "'You shall love the Lord your God with all your heart, and with all your soul, and with all your mind.' This is the greatest and first commandment. And a second is like it: 'You shall love your neighbor as yourself.'"*

(Matthew 22:37–39)

Loving my neighbor as myself implies that I must first know what love is—*and* I must first love myself. Loving myself unconditionally isn't easy. Loving the positive things in my character—my talents and accomplishments—is simple. But I must also love my temper, my stubbornness, and the rest of my faults. When I accept and love *all* of me, I am freed to love another person for all that he or she is.

Joanne M. Tibble
Saint Mary's University of Minnesota
Winona, Minnesota

FOR JUST AS THE BODY IS ONE *and*
has many members, and all the members of the
body, though many, are one body, so it is with
Christ.

(1 Corinthians 12:12)

The magazine shouted from the grocery
   checkout,
"A flat stomach will lead to love:
whittle your waist,
trim your thighs,
hone down those hips."

So, feet shackled in sneakers,
I ran toward the body promised on that
   magazine cover,
toward the promised destination of love.

I found much along that road to the ideal body.
Yes . . . aching legs,
an empty cookie jar,
and the location of the low fat margarine
   in the grocery aisle.

I found fifty new toning exercises for my
   stomach,
a spandex-induced redness around my waist,
and that coupons aren't accepted by fitness
   clubs.
But no—not any love.

Then there was this other book—
the one read from every Sunday
while I sit on my buns of steel.

This book promises love just like the magazine—
but no flat stomach required.

The book tells me I am a part—
not just another curved calf muscle
or bouncing bicep
but a part of another body—the body of Christ.
I don't need a sports bra to know Christ's love.

Just unlatch the window of my heart
and rest in God's sunlight.
Without another rice cake to eat again—ever.

Stephanie Anne Seltzer
Kutztown University
Kutztown, Pennsylvania

FOR I HAVE SET *you an example, that you also should do as I have done to you.*

(John 13:15)

You are my heritage.
You gave me the gifts of your strength, your courage, and the warmth of your heart.
You gave me the sparkle in your eyes that says everything in a glance.
You gave me your heart when you made me your butter cookies, latkas, and homespun magic.
You gave me my sense of dignity and personal integrity.
You gave me the world when you taught me the meaning of generosity.
You taught me to love deeply through your soft touch and warm kisses.
You taught me to serve others when you served me.
You taught me to laugh with your gentle humor.
You gave me everything when you could barely afford to give anything.
You gave me your determined spirit, and you will forever live in my heart and my soul.

For Grandma
Love, Becky

Rebecca Ellen Haines
College Misericordia
Dallas, Pennsylvania

[LOVE] BEARS ALL *things, believes all things, hopes all things, endures all things. Love never ends.*

(1 Corinthians 13:7–8)

It's easy to feel God's loving presence and to be thankful when we are laughing, loving, and dancing with joy—it's harder when we experience sadness and fear. Shining through these difficult times, however, is the bright light of God's love—a love that never fails. It's always there, though sometimes it's hard to recognize.

Throughout my dad's recent diagnosis and battle with leukemia, I felt sadness and fear. It's tempting to give in to these emotions, to stop believing and hoping in love—but that is not the path I intend to take. The path I am taking is lighted with peace, hope, and love—the peace of eternal life in God's loving arms, the hope of tomorrow, the love that gets me through each day: love for my dad, love for life, love for God. If God is love and love never stops believing and hoping, why should I?

Allison
Saint Mary's University of Minnesota
Winona, Minnesota

R<small>EJOICE</small>, *young man, while you are young,*
and let your heart cheer you in the days of your
youth. Follow the inclination of your heart and the
desire of your eyes, but know that for all these
things God will bring you into judgment.

(Ecclesiastes 11:9)

I was born a dreamer, a visionary of exciting
   new possibilities.
Seedling of design that may or may never be,
sprouting hope deep in the bosom of my soul.
Today is the day of the dream,
for tomorrow remains a day out of reach.
Today my dreams may flourish as the ripe vine
   bearing grapes
or wither to despondency, bleached by the sun,
carrying false hopes of joy on tomorrow's
   breath.
Today is the day of the dream.
I have fallen from Eden, eaten of the fruit,
stumbled through the gates of Babylon,
while the vision of the temple floated ahead of
   me unrooted in reality.
Yet today is the day of the dream.
Today I lay the foundation firm, tying my
   dream to reality.
I will tackle that obstacle, for today is the day
   of the dream.
Today my dreams become a reality.

Luke Reisdorf
University of Northern Iowa
Cedar Falls, Iowa

WE KNOW *that all things work together for good for those who love God, who are called according to his purpose.*

(Romans 8:28)

I was having a bad week—it was the first week back after our spring break, and I was overwhelmed by all the work I had to do. And I was sick on top of it. My attitude was not great, either—I was negative and lacking trust in God.

Wednesday came, and along with it, the dreaded chemistry lab, a guaranteed three-hour headache. I had to do my experiment three times to get it done correctly! Of course, I realize that in the big scheme of things, one lab is not life or death, but at the time it felt like my day was going downhill fast.

That night was my Bible study, though, and I debated whether or not I should go because I had a lot of homework and needed extra rest to get well. I decided to go, and am glad I did. We talked about how the week was going for us, and one of the girls said something that really gave my attitude a kick in the rear. She told me to praise God for chemistry lab. . . . Praise God for chemistry lab? This seemed hard to swallow at first—even funny—but then I started to think about it. Who am I to complain about something God has given me? How do I know what God's purposes are? I don't. So why not praise God for everything, good and bad? It certainly helps me to hope and trust in God's plan for me.

Now each time something threatens to annoy or upset me, I try to think to myself, *Praise God* for _____. I challenge you to try it. It's not always easy, but keep at it and it can really make a positive difference.

We see only one tiny part of the picture, but God's vision is larger, and we just need to trust that it is *all*—the darkness and the light—working for our good, if we truly love and praise God for everything.

. . . Yeah, praise God for chemistry lab.

Sarah L. Buck
Marquette University
Milwaukee, Wisconsin

"AND YOU WILL KNOW *the truth, and the truth will set you free.*"

(John 8:32, NAB)

Being honest is not always easy, especially with your parents when you're at college, far from home. Do I tell Mom and Dad that I got wasted last night and woke up in a stranger's apartment? What about honesty with friends? Do I tell him that he really annoys me, or tell her that I need to spend some time alone? What about my professors? Do I cheat on the exam or do my own work?

Take some time and think about whom you are honest with and with whom it is a struggle for you to be honest. I find that being honest with family, friends, and teachers liberates me from further anxieties. It might hurt at times to be truthful, but the reward is always great. If you tell the truth, if you live the truth, you will be set free.

Lord, I pray that I may live a truthful life. Help me to be honest; set me free in your love.

Brian C. Halderman
University of Dayton
Dayton, Ohio

ᴀɴᴅ ʟᴇᴛ ᴛʜᴇ ᴘᴇᴀᴄᴇ *of Christ rule in your hearts, to which indeed you were called in the one body. . . . And be thankful. And whatever you do, in word or deed, do everything in the name of the Lord Jesus, giving thanks to God . . . through him.*

(Colossians 3:15–17)

I owe it all to you—
the life I lead, the air I breathe,
everything . . .
The pain, sorrow, fear,
and the gut-wrenching grief,
without which I never could have felt
the soft, downy touch of love
or the soul-searing bursts of joy.
Every smile I smile, every laugh out loud,
every tear I shed belongs to you.
Every step I take, every decision I make
is guided by your sure, strong hand,
giving me the gentle push I need
when I hesitate.
Every flower that grows,
every living thing in the scope of my world
. . . and beyond . . .
all belong to you,
as do I.

Michelle Marie Colby
Virginia-Maryland Regional College of Veterinary Medicine
Blacksburg, Virginia

[JESUS] SAID, *"Truly I tell you, unless you change and become like children, you will never enter the kingdom of heaven. Whoever becomes humble like this child is the greatest in the kingdom of heaven."*

(Matthew 18:3–4)

What does Jesus mean by these words? What does he mean by "become like children"? My visions of children have chocolaty faces and sticky fingers.

Well, I happen to like chocolate, and sometimes my fingers get sticky, but somehow I don't think this is what Jesus is referring to. . . .

Pondering this, I realized that I had a perspective problem (It's hard to think like a child when you're almost six feet tall!)—and I knew just how to deal with the problem. I got down on my hands and knees, looked around, and said, "Wow, everything is quite different down here. Everything is so big and powerful."

Then, images of children—eyes wide with amazement—flowed into my mind. *This* is it! God wants us to see the wonder in him and everything that he has created.

Megan Meece
University of South Carolina
Columbia, South Carolina

"THEREFORE DO NOT WORRY,
saying, 'What will we eat?' or 'What will we drink?'
or 'What will we wear?' For it is the Gentiles who
strive for all these things. . . . But strive first for
the kingdom of God and his righteousness, and all
these things will be given to you as well."

(Matthew 6:31–33)

God, as a college student, I always worry about
money because I never seem to have enough
of it. Please keep me from desiring material
things—because they do not bring happiness,
and they steer me away from goodness. Let
your love be the sole source of my content.

Jessica J. Trom
Saint Mary's University of Minnesota
Winona, Minnesota

PETER ANSWERED *him, "Lord, if it is you,*
command me to come to you on the water." He
said, "Come." So Peter got out of the boat, started
walking on the water, and came toward Jesus.
But when he noticed the strong wind, he became
frightened, and beginning to sink, he cried out,
"Lord, save me!" Jesus immediately reached out his
hand and caught him, saying to him, "You of little
faith, why did you doubt?"

(Matthew 14:28–31)

I am Peter. You stand before me, Lord, brilliant
calm on the dark, churning sea. I see the love in
your eyes as they search mine; I hear the love
in your voice as you say, "Come." Sure, without
doubts, I rise and walk. Without doubts. A
slight wind swirls around me, distracts me. It
grows stronger—whirling—and stronger. In it
the voices scream, "Delusion! There is no God!
You are alone!" I cannot see you, Lord, I cannot
hear you. Whirl-wind becomes whirlpool,
catching me up, sucking me down. I struggle and
search, murmur weakly, "Lord?" Sinking deeper,
spinning faster, I gasp and claw, "Are you there,
Lord?" Until, overwhelmed by the hopeless
blackness, I give up and am still. I stretch up
my hand and cry out with all my strength,
"Lord! I cannot do it! Save me, please!" Your
strong hand grasps mine, and I am rising.
"Why did you doubt?" you ask. But I cannot
even remember why, so simple and sweet it is to
hold fast to your hand and gaze into your eyes.

Sigrid R. Magid
University of Virginia
Charlottesville, Virginia

MY EYES *are ever toward the* LORD,
for he will pluck my feet out of the net.

(Psalm 25:15)

Jesus,
you felt pain
but did not fear.
You felt sorrow
but did not forget.
You felt free
but did not run away.
I saw your face
and did not fear.
I felt your hand
and did not forget.
I felt free
but did not run away.
I felt your pain,
I felt your sorrow,
I felt free in your arms.
In all of this,
I knew I was not alone.
For it was then that
you protected me from danger,
held me in your arms,
and
lifted me high.
I never felt so loved
until that day
you remembered me
when you left
for your heavenly home.
I did not weep,

for you taught me
just how deep and sincere
your love truly is
for me,
your servant.

Maranda Holt
Saint Mary's University of Minnesota
Winona, Minnesota

"Do not be afraid, *little flock, for it is your Father's good pleasure to give you the kingdom. . . . For where your treasure is, there your heart will be also.*"

(Luke 12:32–34)

Fear is what stops most people from doing the things they want to do in life.

When I first started college, I was afraid of so much—afraid to be alone, afraid to fail in my academics, and afraid of not figuring out what I wanted out of life. I basically lived my life for others, fearing that if I did the things I really wanted to do, no one would like me or understand my reasons. For instance, I started out as a nursing major to please my family, I wore the right clothes to fit in with friends, and I put up with an abusive boyfriend. My life was based on pleasing those around me, not myself.

Things began to change for me this past year as I became more aware of how unhappy I was. I finally got up the nerve to tell my parents about switching my major, and I started wearing the clothes *I* wanted to wear. The abusive boyfriend and I broke up, and to my surprise, I enjoyed being single. My new independence was such a relief compared to my old self-deprived lifestyle.

I'm still changing, and I know it will be a long time until I feel I have hit total self-actualization. I understand now that living in fear of others' opinions is not a healthy way to live; a person has to realize that life has so much more to offer than just what others think.

And this passage from Luke helps me to see that I can do whatever I want in life, no matter what others think. I need to follow what my heart and soul tell me, and this is the ultimate gift a person can give oneself.

Kelly Benson
Viterbo College
La Crosse, Wisconsin

THEN HE SAID to them all, *"If any want to become my followers, let them deny themselves and take up their cross daily and follow me."*

(Luke 9:23)

Lord, I come, offering myself to you.
I give you my mind that I might think
your thoughts;
I give you my eyes that I might see your light;
I give you my ears that I might hear your word;
I give you my mouth that I might speak
your truth;
I give you my hands that I might do your work;
I give you my feet that I might walk
in your ways.
And most of all, Lord,
I give you my shoulders that I might carry
your cross;
I give you my heart that I might love
with your love.
Lord, I give you my life that you might mold me
in your ways
through your mercy and grace.
Lift me up as on the wings of an eagle,
and let me soar in your love and your goodness
till I meet you face-to-face at the waters
of salvation.
Amen!

Robert C. Jones
University of Dayton
Dayton, Ohio

YET, O LORD, *you are our Father;*
we are the clay, and you are our potter;
we are all the work of your hand.

(Isaiah 64:8)

Dear God in heaven, Great Potter of mankind,
Let your loving hands mold me.
Let every groove and curve reflect your work.
Make me durable,
For I know I will take many falls.
Make me useful,
For my life is but to serve.
When I crack or chip,
Mend me anew.
And when I finally break,
Use what I have left behind to mold others.

Meredith Dara Zondag
Viterbo College
La Crosse, Wisconsin

"LISTEN! *A sower went out to sow. And as he sowed, some seed fell on the path, and the birds came and ate it up. . . . Other seed fell into good soil and brought forth grain, growing up and increasing and yielding thirty and sixty and a hundredfold."*

(Mark 4:3–8)

Legacy. This word is often associated with great wealth or estates that are left behind for surviving generations. My great grandmother didn't have either—yet, at her memorial service, the minister remarked about the legacy she left to us. At the time, those remarks seemed strange to me; however, as I reflected upon it, I understood that everyone leaves a legacy. You don't have to be someone like Mother Teresa to have affected people's lives. One never knows—like the sower in Jesus' parable—when the seeds you plant might take root in someone else. This is how we pass on our legacy.

What is your legacy? What thoughts or images or words last in another person's mind after they have spoken with you? Do you leave an impression of your Christianity? What seeds are you planting?

Megan Meece
University of South Carolina
Columbia, South Carolina

BLESSED *are those who trust in the* LORD,
whose trust is the LORD.
They shall be like a tree planted by water,
sending out its roots by the stream.
It shall not fear when heat comes,
and its leaves shall stay green;
in the year of drought it is not anxious,
and it does not cease to bear fruit.
(Jeremiah 17:7–8)

Lord Jesus, make me like the tree, firmly rooted in you and yet bending to the slightest movements of the Holy Spirit, who, like the wind, "blows where it chooses" (John 3:8).

Give me the wisdom to stay where you have put me and to not wander away in search of streams you did not mean for me.

Teach me to be content with my humanity, weary of its own failings and distractions. Help me to embrace the excitement of life without eagerness to be perfect. Help me to face times of aridity without discouragement at my imperfections.

Lord Jesus, be the caretaker of your tree. May its branches give shade to passersby; its fruits nourish the hungry; and its beauty delight the wanderers. May its wood warm strangers in the winter. Amen.

Justyna Braun
Rutgers University
New Brunswick, New Jersey

"WHICH ONE OF YOU, *having a hundred sheep and losing one of them, does not leave the ninety-nine in the wilderness and go after the one that is lost until he finds it?"*

(Luke 15:4)

How many college students would say they feel like a lost sheep? I'll bet it's more than one in ninety-nine: In Luke, Jesus is talking about sinners who stray away . . . but what about us kids who stray off to college? Not that we're fallen-away sinners, but at one time or another, we all feel the loneliness of not belonging. Whether it's the loneliness that comes in the middle of a party, or that hits us as we sit in an empty dorm—most of us are just trying to find our way. After all, that is the point of college, right? Pursuing a career or trying to figure out the meaning of life—we're all looking for something.

So, for all the lost sheep who just can't seem to find their way . . . realize that you've been with the other ninety-nine all along. The Shepherd knows what to do. Let go, and let God work.

Dan Hirsch
DePaul University
Chicago, Illinois

"FOR nothing *will be impossible with God.*" *Then Mary said, "Here am I, the servant of the Lord; let it be with me according to your word."*
(Luke 1:37–38)

Mary, your plans were interrupted and your reputation put at risk. The life you knew and the comfort and security you treasured would be changed for eternity. Yet without hesitation you said, "Yes." I look to you with your complete, spontaneous trust in God and pure submission to God's will—and wonder if I am able to mirror your openness to God. What do I risk? How will my plans be altered?

Strengthen me, God, to submit to you. I place my trust in you, God, to lead me, guide me, love me. For all is possible with you.

Toni M. Riehm
Indiana University South Bend
South Bend, Indiana

"AND WHILE THEY WENT to buy it, the bridegroom came, and those who were ready went with him into the wedding banquet; and the door was shut. Later the other bridesmaids came also, saying, 'Lord, Lord, open to us.' But he replied, 'Truly I tell you, I do not know you.' Keep awake therefore, for you know neither the day nor the hour."

(Matthew 25:10–13)

Procrastination . . . seems that I love it, because I keep procrastinating again and again. Look at me—even this assignment is late! I do not understand why I procrastinate, because every time I do, I get myself into trouble. I might receive a bad grade on a late paper, but more important, I could receive an F in the eyes of God if I keep procrastinating. Thoughts like, "I'll go to church next week" or "I am too tired to pray now so I'll just do it tomorrow" occur all too often.

No one knows when we will be called to the Kingdom of heaven, and if not prepared, we may not be ready to receive God or to find eternal bliss.

Are you ready?

Jodi Lee Bodenberger
Viterbo College
La Crosse, Wisconsin

REJOICE IN THE LORD *always; again I will say, Rejoice. Let your gentleness be known to everyone. The Lord is near. Do not worry about anything, but in everything by prayer and supplication with thanksgiving let your requests be made known to God. And the peace of God, which surpasses all understanding, will guard your hearts and your minds in Christ Jesus.*

(Philippians 4:4–7)

I love the Lord with all my heart.
When all the world crumbles around me
and people disappoint me,
the Lord, my God is always with me.
So I rejoice in God's name, who alone is worthy.
It is through God that I learned the true
meaning of love; it washes over me
day after day,
cleansing me of all Satan's doings.
And because of God's unconditional love
for me,
because of all that's been shown to me,
I can love my brothers and sisters.
The Lord, my God, provides me with everything
I need.
God is my mother, my father, my sister,
God is my brother, my friend, my teacher,
God is my savior.
All I need to do is seek,
and God said I shall find.
There is nothing in this world I fear,
because I trust that God will protect me
and watch over me.

Yes, God can create miracles—the gift of life is
one of them.
And the blessings God gives are
nothing short of amazing.
So I give thanks and praise to the Lord,
my God,
who alone is worthy.
Invite God into your heart
and share what's there.
Give the Lord your love and trust, have faith in
all God does,
and you shall be given something the world
cannot give—
God's everlasting peace.

Sonya Kim
Saint John's University
Jamaica, New York

To you, O Lord, *I lift up my soul.*
  O my God, in you I trust.

I wrote this prayer, and I say it when I am faced
with decisions that boggle my mind, confuse
my heart, and challenge my morals.

God, let me take this moment to listen.
Call out to me your guidance.
Help me find the straight path of life that
      reflects your heart.
Help me make choices that reflect your wisdom.
Help me celebrate the joys you have created.
Help me deal with sorrow by embracing a
      strong faith in you, my God.
Help me live and love fully.
Amen.

Rebecca J. McAulay
Saint Mary's University of Minnesota
Winona, Minnesota

"LOVE YOUR ENEMIES, *do good to those who hate you.*"

(Luke 6:27)

Dear God,
You tell us to love our enemies—for many of us this is the most difficult of all your commandments. Help us each day to remember your ultimate act of kindness and forgiveness. As you hung dying on the cross and your persecutors taunted and mocked you, you asked God in heaven to forgive them. What kind of cruelty have we ever suffered in our life that has been worse than that? Help us to follow your example by not seeking to retaliate when we've been injured by another, but rather to forgive.

Lord, not only do you ask us to love our enemies but also to take it one step further and do good to them. It's hard enough to mentally forgive someone, but you challenge us to show this forgiveness by our outward actions. Again, we need only look to your example to guide us. Many who treated you badly now share eternal life with you in heaven because you are merciful. Lead us to realize that one of the ways we can show our deep love for you is by loving those in our life who may have hurt us the most.

Christine Papke
Viterbo College
La Crosse, Wisconsin

DO YOU NOT KNOW *that your body is a temple of the Holy Spirit within you, which you have from God, and that you are not your own?*

(1 Corinthians 6:19)

The other night my friends and I were having the kind of conversation that can only happen in college—the kind that leaps from topic to topic but always manages to find its way back to sex. They all know I want to wait till I'm married, but that night, for the first time, someone asked me why.

The way I see it, sex isn't a sin, it's a sacrament. God meant sex to be sacred; it's one way we can know—both spiritually and physically—the power of God's love. A physical celebration of the marriage sacrament, sex lets our bodies realize what our hearts already know—that the two have become one.

I want to wait because sex is sacred, not because it's a sin.

Anna M. Johnson
College of William and Mary
Williamsburg, Virginia

"[TEACH] THEM *to obey everything that I have commanded you. And remember, I am with you always, to the end of the age.*"

(Matthew 28:20)

Jesus, you made a promise to always be
    at my side,
Asking me to go out into the world and teach
    the love you've given.
So I venture out, hoping to spread your peace.
I face many trials along the way and rocks that
    threaten to trip me,
But I shall fear no storm, for you have
    authority over rain and thunder.

If I should fall, your grace will lift me up
    above my flaws,
Supporting me through the desert of hard times
    with love.
This dry land can be cruel and uneven, yet still
    you stand beside me,
Holding my hand and lifting me up as a child
    to guard me from the jagged edges.

Jesus, you chose to be human to understand the
    joys and sorrows we all feel,
Enduring the greatest suffering in death to save
    the souls of all people.
In return you only ask for our faith and love,
Wanting us to share your gift of eternal life.

Give us strength to reach out to one another,
Help us heal the suffering of all lands
    and nations,

Guide us through the rugged terrain in which
    we live,
Teach us how to be your love.

Julie Christina Cornett
Ithaca College
Ithaca, New York

"ASK, *and you will receive; seek, and you will find; knock, and the door will be opened to you."*
(Matthew 7:7, REB)

This is a phrase I've learned to embrace. It seems simple enough: "Ask, and you will receive." But it's far from simple.

The first step always seems to be the hardest. Whenever I audition for a play, the hardest thing to do is to get up on stage in front of critical eyes and act. Once I make that first step, everything seems to fall into place; I feel stronger for having "asked," for having "sought," for having "knocked." How can one grow without attempting something new? How can one conquer a fear without stepping up to it and "seeking" to be challenged by it? As I step off the stage, I wish that I was still up there. Although other people fear to do what I have done, I find myself accepting the challenge more and more. I feel like I have conquered as well as grown. Perhaps the role will be mine. . . .

Eric Edward Aschenbrenner
Saint Mary's University of Minnesota
Winona, Minnesota

†HEⅡ HE POURED WATER _into a basin_
and began to wash the disciples' feet and to wipe
them with the towel that was tied around him.
(John 13:5)

When studying to be a nurse, one must learn
how to wash a patient. When I first realized
that this was part of the nursing curriculum, I
immediately dreaded the idea. I thought I could
gladly take care of all other needs of patients,
but washing or bathing another person was too
much to ask. It was when I washed the feet of a
patient for the first time that I began to "see."

I saw the effect on the person I was aiding.
It connected me to her as no words had done
before. She felt renewed, as did I. There was
something so spiritual about it—I could not
place my finger on what it was—it was almost
as if I gave her the utmost respect, empowering
her in a most unusual way.

Let us follow Jesus, then, and be both healer
and servant to one another.

Karla Tramutola
Fairleigh Dickinson University
Teaneck, New Jersey

IF THE SPIRIT of him who raised Jesus from the dead dwells in you, he who raised Christ from the dead will give life to your mortal bodies also through his Spirit that dwells in you.

(Romans 8:11)

Testament

Sailing
the autumn breeze,
a monarch, wings of fire,
settles among the flowers near
the stone.

Alone
here as I am,
such freedom seems the more
remarkable to me, beyond
compare.

Yet, I
dare to believe
that the fallen are raised,
only gaining life eternal
through death.

Michael R. Guerin
Saint John's University
Jamaica, New York

I AM WEARY *with my moaning;*
  every night I flood my bed with tears;
  I drench my couch with my weeping. . . .
Depart from me, all you workers of evil,
  for the LORD has heard the sound of my weeping.
The LORD has heard my supplication;
  the LORD accepts my prayer.

(Psalm 6:6–9)

My time is up here. Four years of my life have
been filled with joy, security, and self-confidence.
But now all I see is uncertainty. A whole new
world is waiting for me, but with no direction it
seems. My path is unclear, and I'm afraid I will
choose the wrong road. The time is approaching when I will have to depend more and more
on myself—and I'm unsure how to handle this.
Do I worry? Should I be nervous? Who will help
me?

  I need not get distressed, but instead pray for
guidance. I will put my hope and faith in the
Lord, who sees my fear and hears me calling for
help. I need the Lord, and I know that with the
Lord listening to me, my uncertainty will fade,
my confidence will return, and my uneasiness
will vanish. I need to believe that I am ready
for the challenges ahead.

C. C.
Saint Mary's University of Minnesota
Winona, Minnesota

THEΠ HE GOT UP *and rebuked the winds and the sea; and there was a dead calm. They were amazed, saying, "What sort of man is this, that even the winds and the sea obey him?"*

(Matthew 8:26–27)

Sometimes I think I'm sinking
It seems my world is crashing down
The tide is coming in too fast
And I'm sure that I'm going to drown
But I behold in the chaos
A ray of hope begin to glow
Because He's coming out to save me
From the stormy seas I know

He's walking on the water
As He whispers, "Peace, be still"
It's faith that leads to safety
When I surrender up my will
His hand is reaching down to me
In the middle of the storm
Then it's He who carries me back home
And keeps me safe and warm

You're drowning in a sea of doubt
Pondering what's wrong and right
You worry all day long
Then cry yourself to sleep at night
But it's He who holds the future
That guides your every move
And it's only when you question Him
That He has to prove

He can still walk on the water
And whisper, "Peace, be still"
It's faith that leads to safety
When you surrender up your will
His hand is reaching down to you
In the middle of the storm
And it's He who carries you back home
And keeps you safe and warm

Clark L. Fabert Jr.
Rockford College
Rockford, Illinois

FOR EVERY SPECIES *of beast and bird, of reptile and sea creature, can be tamed and has been tamed by the human species, but no one can tame the tongue.*

(James 3:7–8)

The tongue is a tiny part of the body, but also one of the most powerful. It can be used to praise or curse God, to bring peace or war. It can create a lasting friendship or, in a moment of anger, end one forever.

Perhaps the most powerful use of the tongue, though, is to spread the Good News of Jesus' love and his death for us on the cross. It is true that no human can tame the tongue, but with God's help, the tongue can be a powerful tool for good. The challenge of these verses from James is to step back and let God use our tongue for the good purposes it was created for. Only then will we be able to truly keep our tongues from evil.

Jennifer Kulzer
Viterbo College
La Crosse, Wisconsin

I CRY ALOUD TO GOD,

aloud to God, that he may hear me.
In the day of my trouble I seek the Lord;
in the night my hand is stretched out without
wearying;
my soul refuses to be comforted. . . .
I meditate and search my spirit:
"Will the Lord spurn forever,
and never again be favorable?
Has his steadfast love ceased forever?
Are his promises at an end for all time?
Has God forgotten to be gracious?
Has he in anger shut up his compassion?"
And I say, . . .
"I will call to mind the deeds of the LORD;
I will remember your wonders of old.
I will meditate on all your work,
and muse on your mighty deeds.
Your way, O God, is holy.
What god is so great as our God?
You are the God who works wonders;
you have displayed your might among the
peoples.

(Psalm 77:1–14)

I like Asaph's prayer. I pray one like it frequently: Dear God, your unfailing love has failed. Your faithfulness missed a spot. You forgot about that need you promised to fulfill. Oops. Scratch that. God, forgive my delusions. How can I doubt your tender mercies that throughout life have been my guide? Recenter my focus on you. Help me to see you in all your glory.

Teach me to seek your Kingdom. You alone are worthy of my praise! Amen.

Missy Graham
Wesleyan College
Macon, Georgia

I CAN DO ALL THINGS *through him who strengthens me.*

(Philippians 4:13)

The test results were finally back—tragedy had struck! My mother was diagnosed with hardening of the arteries and told that she had to have double bypass surgery. How could this be happening? She was too young! Anxiously waiting for the nurse to set up the surgery, I felt tears welling up in my eyes. Was my mother going to die?

My mom, dad, and I went home and talked about the things that needed to be done before she went into the hospital the next morning. Then I shared this verse from Philippians with my mom—it's one I keep in my Bible.

During the surgery this verse kept going through my mind. Finally, we were told that she had made it through surgery and was in recovery. Relieved, I thanked God for letting me keep my mom here with me.

She came home after five days, doing well. Still, that verse stayed in my heart and mind because my faith gave me the strength to get through this. To God I am very grateful!

Diana Kaye Chesser
Saint Catharine College
Saint Catharine, Kentucky

SORROW *is better than laughter,*
because when the face is sad the heart grows wiser.
(Ecclesiastes 7:3, NAB)

Through a series of tragedies, sin, and difficult circumstances, I found that being sad is not all that bad. Many of us have been conditioned to believe that sadness means depression, hopelessness, and defeat. On the contrary, sadness has given me a chance to really let God get to work in my life. Because I am sad, I am weak. Through my weakness I am honest. In my honesty there is faith. By having faith I've allowed God in my heart. While it is true that sadness doesn't always make me feel good, sadness always makes me feel God. So, for that sadness, I have been made glad.

Holy Lord, please continue to move in my life so that I may experience sadness when it is your will, and so appreciate more fully the happier times in life. Amen.

Yolanda Dimitricia White
Alverno College
Milwaukee, Wisconsin

JUST LIKE THE CLAY *in the potter's hand,*
so are you in my hand, O house of Israel.
(Jeremiah 18:6)

God, you formed the Israelites into a great
nation—your people. As you loved and guided
them, direct and shape us into the individuals
that you desire today. May we not be like hard,
dry clay, difficult to be molded—but may we
strive to be like soft clay, willing to be shaped
into the design of the potter. Seeking self-
surrender, may we follow the example of your
Son, Jesus Christ. He followed your will in his
human life and was molded by you to be the
Savior of the world.

Let us work to find the use for which the
potter created us, and always try to fulfill that
purpose.

B. D. Nelson
Saint Mary's University of Minnesota
Winona, Minnesota

[i] will say to the Lord,
"My refuge and my fortress;
my God, in whom I trust."

(Psalm 91:2)

I awoke from my turbulent sleep searching for my glasses. I reached into my hat where the glasses had been stowed for the night, and the relief of discovering my glasses unbroken was short-lived. Once my glasses were on, I could see the contents of my hat—empty! Disbelief commanded my body into a frantic search—where was my fifty-dollar bill?

Gazing into the empty hat, my heart began to ache as I realized that my money truly was gone. On a mission trip, volunteering in the city of Tijuana, doing Gospel-centered work, and missing fifty dollars . . . why me?

I felt myself begin to shut down in frustration and panic. Why was this affecting me this way? Immediately I took my pen, journal, and devotional book and began to do some inner searching. Where do I find refuge? In what or whom do I place trust and seek comfort? I found my answer: true refuge is not in temporal things, like money . . . true refuge is found in the eternal, God!

Anthony C. Holter
Saint Mary's University of Minnesota
Winona, Minnesota

"BLESSED ARE THOSE *who mourn, for*
they will be comforted."

(Matthew 5:4)

For a departed loved one:
Lord, thank you for the time you allowed me to
have with my dearest loved one. Thank you for
the memories, good and bad, that will last a
lifetime. You, Lord, brought us together many
years ago, and I ask you to bring us together
again in your house. I don't understand the
reason why she (he) has been taken away, but
I trust you, Lord; some things are too great to
understand. Lord, please take care of my lost
one, and allow me and her (him) to rest in your
Kingdom together someday. In Christ I pray.
Amen.

Scott Spalding
Saint Catharine College
Saint Catharine, Kentucky

"A DISCIPLE *is not above the teacher, but everyone who is fully qualified will be like the teacher.*"

(Luke 6:40)

Here I wander as a *freshman.*
   I find a path and choose to follow it;
   I find myself in front of tough teachers or
      roadblocks on this path.
Here I sit as a *sophomore.*
   I'm assigned papers of endless length.
   I open my mind to numerous lectures and
      overheads. . . .
Here I push on as a *junior.*
   I begin to wonder if I chose the wrong path?
   Yet through family, friends, and tutors,
   I overcome the roadblocks upon my chosen
      path.
Here I succeed, a *senior.*
   As I receive my diploma, I must stop and
      think,
   I no longer sit in front of teachers but stand
      beside them.
Thank you to my teachers.

Stephanie Anne Persick
Viterbo College
La Crosse, Wisconsin

MY BROTHERS AND SISTERS, *when-ever you face trials of any kind, consider it nothing but joy, because you know that the testing of your faith produces endurance; and let endurance have its full effect, so that you may be mature and complete, lacking in nothing.*

(James 1:2–4)

A college student's life is definitely full of trials, temptations, afflictions, and hardships. Journaling, prayer, and asking the question—Where is God in all of this?—helps me to get through tough times. This question has a profound effect on my spiritual life, keeping me focused on what's most important.

I invite you to reflect on this passage from James when you are facing difficult times in your life or in your spiritual growth. Don't lose sight of where God is in all you are facing.

Malinda Kesteloot
University of Northern Iowa
Fort Dodge, Iowa

SO, WHETHER YOU *eat or drink, or what-*
ever you do, do everything for the glory of God . . .
just as I try to please everyone in everything I do,
not seeking my own advantage, but that of many,
so that they may be saved. Be imitators of me, as I
am of Christ.

(1 Corinthians 10:31—11:1)

Dear heavenly Lord,
As I walk down this slippery road of college life,
riddled with potholes of temptation, I realize
that I cannot make it alone, for I will fall. I ask
that you walk beside me, O Lord, and hold my
hand along the way so that I may stand strong.

   Dear God, please help me to live my life like
the one who died for me, your Son, Jesus Christ.
Help me not to pursue individual gain, but
grant me the grace to do everything for the
greater glory of you. Whether I am in class, at
a party, or in a worship service, allow all my
actions to reflect you. Guide my life so that I
may be a witness, sharing the Gospels with
others. I thank you for your merciful blessings.
In your dear Son Jesus Christ's name, I pray.
Amen.

Zachary S. Mabe
Catawba College
Salisbury, North Carolina

MAY THE GOD OF HOPE *fill you with all joy and peace in believing, so that you may abound in hope by the power of the Holy Spirit.*

(Romans 15:13)

College is supposed to be the best time
    of our life.
But with it comes homework, tests, papers,
    deadlines,
Extracurricular activities, resumes,
Side jobs, grades, expectations, challenges,
Obstacles, and dreams.

To live up to those dreams and to hurdle those
    obstacles of
Everyday college life,
We must have one ingredient: Hope.
Hope to build our future, to strive to do
    our best,
To succeed in college and beyond,
And sometimes hope just to pass that test.
With hope comes believing in yourself:
We need to believe we can do it, to take
    the extra step,
And to know we are building
A successful future for ourselves.

By attending college, we took the first step to
Achieve our dreams.
With hope and with belief in ourselves,
We will be successful in college and beyond.

Kimberly Anne Gabryel
Saint Joseph's College
Rensselaer, Indiana

SO PETER GOT OUT *of the boat, started walking on the water, and came toward Jesus. But when he noticed the strong wind, he became frightened, and beginning to sink, he cried out, "Lord, save me!" Jesus immediately reached out his hand and caught him.*

(Matthew 14:29–31)

Every time I hear these words, I am amazed. How is it that Peter was able to walk on water? I'll admit that when I was young, I attempted to walk on water in a few hotel pools. It never worked, but I kept trying. It is so easy to lose that kind of childlike faith and become focused on human limitations. Yet, when we are totally focused on God, we can break free from those limitations and accomplish amazing things. We must believe we can. Like Peter, we fail only when we doubt God's power.

L. A. C.
Saint Mary's University of Minnesota
Winona, Minnesota

Trust in the Lord *with all your heart,*
  and do not rely on your own insight.
In all your ways acknowledge him,
  and he will make straight your paths.

(Proverbs 3:5–6)

I was given this Bible passage on a little "Bible keepsake" from my mother when I was about fifteen years old. On the back of the keepsake, the woman who designed it wrote that her mother had died when she was very young, and that her grandmother had given her the passage to soothe her heart. This touched me very deeply.

Whenever I feel that things are not going as I expect or want, I say the passage in my mind, comforted by the thought that I don't have to worry so much about where I am going in life or what I will do. I just trust that if I acknowledge God, I will be led to where I am meant to be.

College is filled with stress, and it can seem like a battle against time that you have no control over. When I pause to recall this passage from Proverbs, I calm down and am able to put things into perspective.

Jennifer Duckwitz
Viterbo College
La Crosse, Wisconsin

"COME TO ME, *all you that are weary and are carrying heavy burdens, and I will give you rest. Take my yoke upon you, and learn from me; for I am gentle and humble in heart, and you will find rest for your souls."*

(Matthew 11:28–29)

There are many times when you feel
great despair
Problems seem to escalate and seem
too hard to bear
The pain becomes great and doesn't seem
to go away
It feels like a constant fight just to make it
through each day

It is at these times you must trust
that Jesus is here
Because he loves you and he truly does care
He will stretch out his hand to you
And he will give the strength you need
to make it through
His love for you cannot even be put to measure
You are more precious than gold, and you are
his greatest treasure

Jennifer Marie Kohrman
Indiana University, Purdue University
Fort Wayne, Indiana

HATRED *stirs up strife,*
but love covers all offenses.

(Proverbs 10:12)

Hatred is the epitome of all evil in the world today. To hate is to turn away from God. Conflict can breed pain and misery if not handled with love.

Hatred is the darkness that may be a part of my life, but there is always a way out of the darkness through Jesus, the light of the world. His love will take away the pain and will warm the coldness in my heart. Love is like a warm blanket that I can have with me always—if I believe and have faith—because God is love. If I have God in my life, then I will also have love in my life. Love soothes and comforts the wounds that hatred creates. With the love of Jesus, hatred vanishes and love abounds.

Lord, may I learn to love as you do—unconditionally—so that I may erase hatred from my vocabulary and from my very existence. May I be a more peaceful, loving, and trusting child of God. May I share your love with others, and may your light shine through me forever.

Melissa J. Meyer
Viterbo College
La Crosse, Wisconsin

İn †HA† REΠEWAL *there is no longer Greek and Jew, circumcised and uncircumcised, barbarian, Scythian, slave and free; but Christ is all and in all! . . . And let the peace of Christ rule in your hearts, to which indeed you were called in the one body. And be thankful.*

(Colossians 3:11–15)

Red and yellow
black and white
one body
hand in hand.

Joy and peace
faith and love
pour out
across the land.

Needy and afflicted
anxious and alone
are welcomed
by the wise.

Praise and prayer
faith and friendship
have power
to open eyes.

Alpha and Omega
God and Creator
a promise
to us all.

Shouts and whispers
reach and beckon
God is
our daily call.

Jan Loudin
Fairmont State College
Fairmont, West Virginia

TEACH ME your way, O LORD,
that I may walk in your truth;
give me an undivided heart to revere your name.
I give thanks to you, O Lord my God, with my
whole heart,
and I will glorify your name forever.
(Psalm 86:11–12)

These psalm verses are from a prayer of David, a prayer in time of distress. I pray them as part of my morning prayer so as to rededicate myself each day (stressful or not) to God and God's ways. Setting the proper framework within which to live a Christian life, these words act as a daily course correction for me.

Dennis A. Dziekan
University of Cincinnati
Cincinnati, Ohio

FAITHFUL FRIENDS *are a sturdy shelter:*
whoever finds one has found a treasure.

(Sirach 6:14)

This exhortation is dedicated to my friends.

N. M.—Your **N**urturing and **M**indful discernment give me direction in certain situations.

F. B.—Your **F**rankness and **B**oldness bring out the best in me.

M. G.—Your "**M**ickness" and **G**enerosity make me feel important.

N. C.—Your **N**oble and **C**aring character purifies my heart to be compassionate and loving like our Redeemer.

J. H.—Your **J**ustice and **H**umility prove your high ideals in life, which I uphold.

M. S.—Your **M**aturity and **S**incerity in living life's journey lead me to God's right path.

Thank you, Lord, for blessing me with special friends that make my life ALIVE.

Marc Garcia
Saint John's University
Jamaica, New York

MY BROTHERS AND SISTERS, *whenever you face trials of any kind, consider it nothing but joy, because you know that the testing of your faith produces endurance; and let endurance have its full effect, so that you may be mature and complete, lacking in nothing.*

(James 1:2–4)

I was totally stunned. How could my father be suffering so much? How could his lungs, kidneys, and liver all have stopped at the same time? I had to leave. I had to find some reassuring words that would somehow make the pain go away. Faith had been easy just thirty minutes ago. . . .

I grabbed the nearest book and began to read. Within minutes my eyes came upon this passage from James. As much as I wanted to, I could not find joy in the fact that my dad had very little chance of living. And it felt like facing this test was beyond my ability. But then I realized that if I didn't trust in God's grace, I would never make it. I began to trust, and I was helped—it wasn't easy, but I learned about endurance. Dad's enduring just fine, too.

Daniel James Olsen
Saint Mary's University of Minnesota
Winona, Minnesota

*T*URN *T*O *M*E *and be gracious to me,*
  for I am lonely and afflicted.
Relieve the troubles of my heart,
  and bring me out of my distress.
Consider my affliction and my trouble,
  and forgive all my sins.
Consider how many are my foes,
  and with what violent hatred they hate me.
                    (Psalm 25:16–19)

When it seems that all the world is against you,
    When it seems that you are all alone,
        Come to Love.

        When life appears too hard,
        When life appears too long,
            Come to Love.

        Come to Love,
    And Love will be on your side.
    Love will never leave you.
    Love will see you through.
        Come back to Love.
            Come.

                              Jeffry Lusiak
              Saint Mary's University of Minnesota
                      Winona, Minnesota

[JESUS] ENTERED *Jericho and was passing through it. A man was there named Zacchaeus; he was a chief tax collector and was rich. He was trying to see who Jesus was, but on account of the crowd he could not, because he was short in stature. So he ran ahead and climbed a sycamore tree to see him, because he was going to pass that way.*

(Luke 19:1–4)

There are many ways to see Jesus' face today. We can see it when we help other people, and when we are being helped. We can see it in a smile, a caring face, or a hug.

I saw Jesus in the face of a very devout girl. I loved being around her because I felt Jesus working through her. However, she moved away after graduating, and we grew apart. I was lonely, and I wondered how—without her—I could ever see Jesus' face again. I asked God to send someone into my life who could show me the face of Jesus. As the weeks passed, I grew lonelier. I believed that Jesus would always be with me, but I felt as if I were alone.

Then one day while reading a book about Mother Teresa, I noticed how often she talked about seeing the face of Jesus while working among the poorest of the poor. I began to understand that Jesus *is* out there, but I must be willing to do what it takes to see him—even if it means climbing a sycamore tree.

James C. Settles
West Texas A & M University
Canyon, Texas

†HEN MARY SAID, *"Here am I, the*
servant of the Lord; let it be with me according to
your word." Then the angel departed from her.
(Luke 1:38)

Whenever I hear your story, O Mother of God,
I am touched and strengthened.
You were able to set aside your fears and doubts
    to obey God;
Your faith pulled you through and gave you
    strength.
You said yes to God even though you were
    alone and unsure.
When life gets me down, or my tasks seem
    impossible,
I think of you and know that nothing is
    impossible with God.
You help me to realize that God really will
    provide,
And will look out for me all the days of my life.
Your example of faith and trust guides me to
    Christ,
And you will forever be my beloved Mother,
    Mother to all life.

Jodie Rebecca Marianna Gilfeather
Elizabethtown College
Elizabethtown, Pennsylvania

Do not LOVE SLEEP, *or else you will*
come to poverty;
open your eyes, and you will have plenty of bread.
(Proverbs 20:13)

At times I look only at the negative side of life—such as, when I have a great workload ahead or when things don't go right. It can be easier to fall into negativity than to deal with what is ahead.

I have heard, God, that you will not give a person more than he or she can handle, and I have to admit, sometimes I find this hard to believe. Help me remember that everything will get done, and that being negative will not make it go faster or easier.

Trisha Jean Reichenberger
Saint Mary's University of Minnesota
Winona, Minnesota

But Mary stood *weeping outside the tomb.*

(John 20:11)

Mary Magdalene stood weeping at the tomb; she knew instinctively that there was nowhere else to go. She had lost the one whom she loved, and there was no consolation for her anywhere in the world. Mary, who had experienced an overwhelming, deeply abiding love for Jesus, now was shattered and engulfed by the searing pain of loss. There was no relief. As intense as her love had been, her pain now shared the same depth.

There was no relief for Mary because her pain and her love originated from the same source. Both pointed her toward the One she loved, and who had been taken from her sight. She had to learn to recognize him again, to hear his voice calling her name.

The dark curtain of death seems to separate us from the ones we love, perhaps even from the God who holds them. God longs to tear open that curtain, but does so slowly—in gentle memories and the gradual recognition that we and they abide forever, unseparated, in one place—the heart of God, who loves them and us far beyond our imagining.

Ann M. Michaud
Weston Jesuit School of Theology
Cambridge, Massachusetts

İ WİLL GİVE THAΠKS *to the* LORD *with my*
whole heart;
  I will tell of all your wonderful deeds.
I will be glad and exult in you;
  I will sing praise to your name, O Most High.
                                      (Psalm 9:1–2)

I thank the Lord every day for blessing me with
a new day of life, a loving family, and a remarkable girlfriend who has made my life
complete. My life might not be perfect, but I
wouldn't trade what I have for anything in this
world. My mother taught me to be thankful for
what I have, because there are people out there
who are less fortunate and would love to live in
my shoes. Friends, be thankful for what you
have been given.

Josh Newton
Saint Catharine College
Saint Catharine, Kentucky

JACOB WAS LEFT ALONE; *and a man wrestled with him until daybreak. . . . So he said to him, "What is your name?" And he said, "Jacob." Then the man said, "You shall no longer be called Jacob, but Israel, for you have striven with God and with humans, and have prevailed."*
(Genesis 32:24–28)

Struggle and difficulty are crucibles of transformation; trial and tribulation are furnaces in which we forge our own personal identity. Because he wrestled with an angel, Jacob received a new name; he gained a new identity and was transformed into a new creature.

Similarly, when we wrestle with the quandaries that life places before us, we are transformed. When we face squarely and evenly the many dilemmas that arise within the course of a lifetime, our response to those dilemmas show us who we truly are. For those of us who strive to follow the path of self-knowledge and self-awareness, it might be worthwhile to take a moment and consider: How have I responded to the various struggles in which I have found myself, and what do those responses say about who I am?

Robert Horihan
Saint Mary's University of Minnesota
Winona, Minnesota

"GIVE THANKS *in all circumstances; for this is the will of God in Christ Jesus for you.*"

(1 Thessalonians 5:18)

Dear heavenly God,

Thank you for another beautiful day. I pray that I might be able to take to heart, today and forevermore, these words from Paul—because you are so worthy, God, and you have blessed me abundantly.

I praise you for letting me grow closer to you in college. I know many who have drifted away from you during this time of independence, and I am grateful to know that you are always by my side. In an age where everything seems transient, it is wonderful to know that you alone are the ever present and everlasting master of my soul.

Let me forever walk in your ways and never stray from your path. Continue to kindle the unquenchable fire within me to seek you daily, worship you in every waking moment, and keep you at the center of my life.

In your sweet and holy name I pray. Amen.

Jennifer J. Ng
Cornell University
Ithaca, New York

No testing *has overtaken you that is not common to everyone. God is faithful, and he will not let you be tested beyond your strength, but with the testing he will also provide the way out so that you may be able to endure it.*

(1 Corinthians 10:13)

Today's western culture leaves us with no shortage of temptations, to be certain. In a time so driven by unworthy desires, it can be difficult to avoid the temptations of greed and lust and indulgence, which bring only fleeting happiness.

To truly find peace is to find our rewards in the teachings of Jesus. Because he loves us, he will be there in times of need when we feel pressured to indulge in dishonest academic behaviors, drugs, immoral sexual activity, or anything else that harms others. For when we harm others, we harm God.

At times it takes incredible strength to withstand even the slightest temptations, but if we have faith and pray when we are distressed, God will answer us and give us the strength we need. All is possible through God.

Jessica
Viterbo College
La Crosse, Wisconsin

LET US THEN LAY ASIDE *the works of darkness and put on the armor of light.*

(Romans 13:12)

Saint Paul calls us to cultivate within ourselves the radiance of Christ, the Light of the World. We are gifted with the fire of Christ's boundless love burning inside us. There is no greater love than this, no light that burns brighter. Even in our dark times and our sinfulness, Christ is present, waiting to touch us with a gentle hand of mercy, wipe our tears away, and bring us back to the light. We enkindle the love of Christ inside us by doing as Jesus did—giving of ourselves to others and loving one other. When we enlighten ourselves with Christ's love, the possibilities are endless; the light of Christ is never extinguished.

Andrea Santoriello
College of the Holy Cross
Worcester, Massachusetts

THE LORD *is your guardian;*
  the LORD is your shade
  at your right hand.
By day the sun cannot harm you,
  nor the moon by night.
The LORD will guard you from all evil,
  will always guard your life.
The LORD will guard your coming and going
  both now and forever.

                              (Psalm 121:5–8, NAB)

Lord God,
You are my guardian.
My faith in you is my shield.
Do not just guard but guide as well.
In this time of uncertain directions—
decisions about my future—
guard me and guide me
to make the right choices.
Guide me to make my path of life straight
to a place of true peace.
Guard it as you guard the straight path that
leads you into my heart and my soul. Amen.

                              Eric Andrew Morse
                              Drake University
                              Des Moines, Iowa

"TODAY, *if you hear his voice,
do not harden your hearts as in the rebellion.*"
(Hebrews 3:15)

Once in a while, I find myself stumbling through life, forgetting that I have given God permission to direct me.

When I started back to school in the fall, I took some time to remind God of all the different activities that were pulling at my hectic schedule.

"Let's make a deal, God. Since I have a family, I volunteer at church, I attend extracurricular activities to support the school, I make good grades, *and* I offer a nice smile in the hallway—how about you don't ask me to get involved with or minister to any *new* people while I'm trying to get this education."

As I walked into my first class, my eyes were immediately drawn to a woman in the front row. I almost heard the chuckle of my "director," guiding me to the seat next to her and whispering, "This person needs a friend and I choose *you!*"

Lord, thank you for the confidence you place in me to tell others about you. Please teach me to listen. Amen.

Margaret Tyler
Missouri Valley College
Marshall, Missouri

"LOVE YOUR ENEMIES, *do good to those who hate you.*"

(Luke 6:27)

Dear God,
You have given me great love;
it is burning deep within—
within my body, my heart, my soul.
Please give me the strength to
keep an open mind,
to give this love even to those I hate—
as you have taught us.

Andrea Kay Nelson
Viterbo College
La Crosse, Wisconsin

"'FOR I WAS HUNGRY *and you gave me food, I was thirsty and you gave me something to drink, I was a stranger and you welcomed me, I was naked and you gave me clothing, I was sick and you took care of me, I was in prison and you visited me.'"*

(Matthew 25:35–36)

One memory of my semester in Italy that I will keep with me forever is of the gypsies who sit in doorways of churches and beg for handouts. I never knew how to respond to them, because my language skills were limited, and my knowledge of "the system" they lived under was more limited still.

It was easy to see that the gypsies were the hungry, the thirsty, the strangers, the naked, the ill, and the imprisoned whom Jesus calls us to reach out to. Back at college, I meet people who have a different, less obvious kind of hunger and imprisonment. That person who sits next to me in class might really need to vent about what's going on with her roommate, or maybe the guy ahead of me in the cafeteria is having megadifficulties with his parents. How can I reach out to Jesus within the people that I come into contact with every day? This is the real challenge that Christ gives us.

Tracy Klassen
Saint Mary's University of Minnesota
Winona, Minnesota

BUT THOSE WHO WAIT *for the Lord*
  shall renew their strength,
  they shall mount up with wings like eagles,
they shall run and not be weary,
  they shall walk and not faint.

(Isaiah 40:31)

A dear friend of mine sent this passage to me when a lump was discovered on my thyroid. Because of her unconditional love and support, along with the support of my family and friends, I was able to get though a very difficult time in my life. I had to trust in God, stop worrying about all the "what ifs," and focus on what was in front of me—a loving family and devoted friends that would stand by me, whatever may come. . . . So I offered up all my worries and let God take care of them. God did, and I'm doing just fine.

Amy Jo Miller
Iowa State University
Ames, Iowa

FOR NOW WE SEE *in a mirror, dimly, but then we will see face to face. Now I know only in part; then I will know fully, even as I have been fully known. And now faith, hope, and love abide, these three; and the greatest of these is love.*
(1 Corinthians 13:12–13)

Faith is the virtue that brings me to believe in you, God, and all your mysteries. Although faith is unseen knowledge, teach me, God, to trust and accept you in my life. I will come to fully understand your mysteries when I come to meet you in paradise. Then I will seek answers to questions I cannot ask now. Help me, God, to live my faith and to respond to your call.

Hope allows me to live through sorrows and joys. Open my heart and mind to you, God, so that I may find the gift of hope. May I not fear times of loneliness and trouble. Every sunset symbolizes another day for which virtuous hope helps me survive.

Love is all around us and in everything that we do. Our life is surrounded by your love, and we extend that love to others. Virtue of virtues, of which love is the greatest; everyone needs love, therefore everyone needs you, Creator of all things and source of all love.

Jennifer Marie Novak
Saint Mary's University of Minnesota
Winona, Minnesota

"COME, *let us return to the LORD.*"

(Hosea 6:1)

It is never too late to turn to God. It is never too late to ask for God's forgiveness.

When I was in fourth grade, my grandma died. Having been very close to her, I was angry with God when she died. I wrote a letter to my grandma telling her I would never forgive God—and I would miss her always. My letter was buried with her.

As time went on, my anger toward God faded. I realized that it was easier to pray to God than to continue being angry. The irony is that my letter was buried—both literally and figuratively.

A time comes for most of us when we want to turn away from God. But hopefully—one day—we want to go back. God is there for us through it all.

One of my favorite bumper stickers reads If you're headed in the wrong direction, God allows U-turns.

Jennifer Tracy
Saint Mary's University of Minnesota
Winona, Minnesota

THERE IS NO FEAR *in love, but perfect love casts out fear.*

(1 John 4:18)

I realized today—I don't want you to die.
It was something about the sermon and I was
thinking of my grandmother
and I was thinking, I couldn't do what she does.
I don't want you to die.
I can't imagine my life without you now.
Before I met you—
I would walk to church, walk to my classes,
walk to swim practice—alone
and I would take pride in that.
But I can't imagine ever being that person again.
Now, when I walk by myself or ride my bike or
have a long, horrible kick set—
I think of what you might be doing or what you
might be thinking—
and I'm not alone anymore.
I'm glad Megan introduced me to you.
I'm glad I was brave and sat down next to you.
I'm glad I know your middle name.

I just wanted you to know all this—
I got really scared in church today.
I don't want anything bad to happen to you—
ever.
Death is terrifying, and terrible.
I hope I can face it with you.

Krista Maren Puttler
Northwestern University
Evanston, Illinois

"This is my commandment, *that you love one another as I have loved you."*

(John 15:12)

My brother and I have never been really close. I'd try to push my way in, he would ease the door open a little—then suddenly slam it in my face. He would say such hurtful things, and my first reaction would be to lash out, to make him hurt like I was hurting. When this pattern became too emotionally draining, I decided to close my own door; I didn't speak to him for months. If he didn't want my love, fine; but it was too painful to keep getting my hand—and my heart—slammed in the door. That was just too much to ask . . . wasn't it?

I began to think about how Jesus loves us. We despised, mocked, betrayed, tortured, and killed him. How he must have been tempted at times to snap his fingers, go back to heaven, and be done with us! But he drew so deeply from God's infinite love that he was able to love us unconditionally, knowing that all he needed he received from God.

Jesus, thank you for never closing the door on me, no matter how unworthy and ungrateful I am! Teach my stubborn heart, I pray, that no love is ever too much to ask.

Sigrid R. Magid
University of Virginia
Charlottesville, Virginia

AND SUDDENLY *there was with the angel a multitude of the heavenly host, praising God and saying,*
>*"Glory to God in the highest heaven,*
>>*and on earth peace among those whom he favors!"*

(Luke 2:13–14)

Gloria

A song that has awakened the dead,
>dispelled the darkness.

Light that illuminates a new people
>as God has illuminated my soul.

Stephanie T. Roberts
Towson University
Towson, Maryland

THEN PETER CAME *and said to him, "Lord, if another member of the church sins against me, how often should I forgive? As many as seven times?" Jesus said to him, "Not seven times, but, I tell you, seventy-seven times."*

(Matthew 18:21–22)

My sister could never stay angry for long. The situation usually started like this: I said something that offended her. Then a war of words developed. The fight always climaxed with my sister saying, "I will never ever play with you again! I will never *talk* to you again." And with this she would storm out of the room. After years of experience, her words never bothered me though, because I knew that she would be back in two minutes, saying, "I'm bored. What do you want to play?"

I have always aspired to be able to forgive like my sister; however, I tend to need more than two minutes. I never asked what my sister did in those two minutes to completely forgive and forget the situation.

Take the next couple of minutes to reflect on what—and who—you have left unforgiven.

Megan Meece
University of South Carolina
Columbia, South Carolina

"TEACHER, *do you not care that we are perishing?" He woke up and rebuked the wind, and said to the sea, "Peace! Be still!" Then the wind ceased, and there was a dead calm. He said to them, "Why are you afraid? Have you still no faith?"*

(Mark 4:38–40)

Lord Jesus, you have the power to control the wind and the sea, and yet, how often do I—like your Apostles as they were crossing the Sea of Galilee—lack trust in your powerful presence? If you are able to control the elements of the earth, surely you are able to calm the storms that disturb the waters of my soul. Grant me, Lord Jesus, the faith to trust in your calming presence in my boat as I cross the Sea of Life. May I feel reassured that you will not let your servant drown under waves of fear and hopelessness; and may I be at peace knowing that together we will reach the happy shores of your Kingdom. Amen.

Tait Schroeder
Saint Mary's University of Minnesota
Winona, Minnesota

In ALL YOUR WAYS *acknowledge him,*
and he will make straight your paths.

(Proverbs 3:6)

One Sunday during Mass at my home parish, the priest was blessing the bread as we all knelt attentively. In the back of the church sat an old phone that was never used. The priest paused, held the blessed bread upward—when suddenly the phone began to ring, echoing loudly through the church. The parishioners looked at one another, wondering what to do—that phone had never rung before. The priest continued on with Communion.

I started thinking about the power of God. What if it was God calling? Nobody answered it—and we know it probably wasn't God on the other end—but the ringing phone sure grabbed everyone's attention.

At one time or another, we experience the call of God in our life. Are we paying attention? Are we listening? Will we risk answering?

Rebecca J. McAulay
Saint Mary's University of Minnesota
Winona, Minnesota

HOW LONG, *O LORD? Will you forget me forever?*
How long will you hide your face from me?
How long must I bear pain in my soul,
*   and have sorrow in my heart all day long?*
How long shall my enemy be exalted over me?
*   (Psalm 13:1–2)*

Grief will not crowd my thoughts,
Sorrow will not invade my soul
Because of you, Lord.

No anguish is greater than your love for me.
The love my latent heart learns to welcome—
A gift from you, Lord.

The gift makes your way known to me.
Can I help others find your way
With help from you, Lord?

Can we live life so simply amid sorrow and fear?
Can we spread joy while engulfed by pain?
Will we give love
To those who have not welcomed you,
To those who have not welcomed us,
Or will we lose hope along with them?

So simple, so pure is your love.
So clouded, so unsure is ours
When it confronts anyone but you.
But you are in everyone.
We will begin to confront you, Lord.

Susanne Quarfoth
Saint Mary's University of Minnesota
Winona, Minnesota

İ HAVE FOUGHT† *the good fight, I have finished the race, I have kept the faith.*

(2 Timothy 4:7)

I have failed often in my life. Sometimes, when in the thick of failure, I wonder why I even bother. Why keep trying things I know I will never be able to do?

W. C. Fields once said, "If at first you don't succeed, try, try again. Then quit. No use being a fool about it." I sure am glad that Peter didn't have this same attitude. Peter was the only one brave enough to jump out of the boat and walk to Jesus; but didn't he lose faith and begin to sink? Didn't Peter fall asleep in the Garden of Gethsemane while Jesus prayed? Although Peter professed Jesus to be Christ, didn't he deny Jesus three times later on? Hearing the cock crow, it could have been easy for Peter just to give up: Why bother? I will always be a sinner. I can't win this fight.

But Peter knew that when fighting the good fight, he would get knocked down sometimes. He understood that while running the race, he might stumble. He also believed, however, that through Christ all things are possible. Christ was the reason Peter kept the faith. Christ was the reason Peter never gave up.

James C. Settles
West Texas A & M University
Canyon, Texas

AGAIN JESUS SPOKE *to them, saying, "I am the light of the world. Whoever follows me will never walk in darkness but will have the light of life."*

(John 8:12)

God, you are the light of the world.
Look down on your children
    with love and mercy.
Use your light to guide us to the path that
You have set aside in our name.
Keep us from being blinded by the glory
    of your light; rather,
Burn away the darkness that lies in our path
    and keeps us from you.

Grant that we might find comfort in the
    midst of adversity, and
Allow us to use our suffering as wood
    for the fire that burns within.
Let us use the light of life you have so
    graciously given us
To spread your word, the message of your love,
To all who remain in darkness,
So that we might try to repay you
For the wonderful gifts you have given us,
And give you glory and praise forever and ever.
Amen.

Dave West
University of Oklahoma
Norman, Oklahoma

AПYOПE WHO TILLS *the land will have*
plenty of bread,
but one who follows worthless pursuits will have
plenty of poverty.

(Proverbs 28:19)

God, help me remember that my days on Earth
are precious and numbered. Please do not let
me waste my time doing useless things. Inspire
me to live each day to its fullest potential so
that it may be seen as worthy in your eyes.

Jessica J. Trom
Saint Mary's University of Minnesota
Winona, Minnesota

I CAN DO ALL THINGS *through him who strengthens me.*

(Philippians 4:13)

There was a time when I questioned the truth of this passage. My version went like this: I can do all things through *Julie,* who has enough strength.

Living through some tough experiences, including college, I discovered that alone, I do not have enough strength. God, on the other hand, has more than enough. Usually I did not ask God for strength to face the challenges I met; and when I did ask, it seemed that God's plan did not fit my plan. I've tasted failure, but I've also matured and grown in understanding. Now I feel God's almighty strength—and I need it.

Friend, do not be afraid to ask for God's strength. Be patient and trusting when it seems like the answers you hoped for aren't the ones you receive. In time you will know God's peace and comfort if you have faith. God is more than willing to help—be willing to accept God's help. Then, all things can be done because you are letting God strengthen you.

Julie Settles
Saint Catharine College
Saint Catharine, Kentucky

ᛏHEᏐ ᏠESUS, *crying with a loud voice, said,*
"Father, into your hands I commend my spirit."
Having said this, he breathed his last.

(Luke 23:46)

We crucified him.
I looked up to my Jesus hanging on the cross.
He was crying, not for himself but for us.
The man I called brother, who shared a meal
        with me,
He is crucified, and we all carry the guilt.

We crucified him.
He called me to be a disciple.
I replied, *"Surely not I, Lord?"* but I followed.
He came to wash my feet.
I replied, *"Surely not I, Lord?"* but I allowed it.
Someone called me a follower of my Lord,
I replied, *"Surely not I?"*—then I wept.
I helped crucify him.

We crucified him.
As here hangs my salvation,
my head hangs as low as the cross hangs high.
And as I kiss the cross, my tears wash his feet
as he had washed mine.
He looked at me from the top of the cross,
and said, "Don't cry, I am always with you."
I replied, *"Surely not I, Lord?"*—we crucified you.
He smiled, and breathed his last.

We crucified him.

Stephanie T. Roberts
Towson University
Towson, Maryland

"So I say to you, Ask, and it will be given you; search, and you will find; knock, and the door will be opened for you. For everyone who asks receives, and everyone who searches finds, and for everyone who knocks, the door will be opened."
(Luke 11:9–10)

There I was, the whole world at my feet, and I—barely six years old, with scabby knees and chocolate popsicle stains streaking the front of my shirt—could be anything I dreamed of. High-top sneakers stuck with friendship pins scraped lightly against the tree bark as my small body swung to and fro from raw fingertips gripping the highest possible branch. With leaves in my mass of stringy brown tangles and wind wrapping my skin in the blanket of the summer heat, all problems were forgotten.

Now as my Icelandic finals approach, my thoughts often turn to those childhood memories. I went abroad looking for something inside myself—something I couldn't find within the bustle of everyday life. I'm terrified. I am alone, I am unprepared, and I am not even sure what I am searching for. But deep inside of me, a voice resounds: "Ask, search, knock."

The Icelandic trees leave a lot to be desired, but I know that throughout my life, God is always with me, swinging from the branches by my side and whispering his messages into the blanket of the summer winds . . . ask, search, knock . . . you will find your answers.

Rebekah Skoor
Fjölbrautaskólinn vid Armúla
Reykjavik, Iceland

SURELY GOODNESS *and mercy*
shall follow me
all the days of my life.

(Psalm 23:6)

As I walk down this path of life
Narrow as the razor's edge
And dark as night with uncertainty
I ask that you grant me the knowledge
    to keep my faith

My Lord I do not know where my life
    will lead me
But if it is with you I shall not fear
Even if I do not always have understanding
I do have comfort
For my faith rests in you

For this I thank you
And for this I pray to you
Help me keep my faith

Daniel Rech
Saint Mary's University of Minnesota
Winona, Minnesota

PUT THESE THINGS *into practice, devote*
yourself to them, so that all may see your progress.
Pay close attention to yourself and to your teaching;
continue in these things, for in doing this you will
save both yourself and your hearers.

(1 Timothy 4:15–16)

How can we find time amid all the craziness of
college life to attend to ourselves and God?
Make a date. I'm serious! Call God up (God is
so hi-tech you don't even need a phone!), open
your calendar, and make a date to do dinner,
go for a walk, swing at nighttime—anything. I
don't believe God cares what you do together;
God just longs to spend time with you. And I
believe that God loves to have fun! The key is—
write it down in your calendar and stick with it.
Be true to your promise to spend that time with
God. Time with God is the best-spent time you
can have—besides, how could you have a better
date?

Sheri Rugg
University of Arizona
Tucson, Arizona

"INDEED, *it is easier for a camel to go through the eye of a needle than for someone who is rich to enter the kingdom of God.*"

(Luke 18:25)

Say, what?
Camel? Needle?
Yeah, right.
Thank God, I'll never be rich.
Sure my future vision holds
a good paying job,
a nice car,
some money in the bank,
maybe an entertainment system.
But rich?
No.
I won't be counted among the rich.
Wait a minute . . .
job
car
bank account
entertainment system

What does that camel have to do again?

Ann B. Schinderle
Viterbo College
La Crosse, Wisconsin

Now the word of the Lord

came to me saying, "Before I formed you in the womb I knew you, and before you were born I consecrated you; I appointed you a prophet to the nations."

(Jeremiah 1:4–5)

That night Francina blurted out: "I'm pregnant. And I have an appointment at an abortion clinic tomorrow." I could not believe my ears. Francina and I had discussed abortion often and had agreed on our stance: It was wrong. Now Francina was telling me she was going to have one tomorrow!

Together, we read these words from Jeremiah, and I told her: "This says to me that God knows us from the very beginning, and has a plan for each person. That is why I think you should have this baby." I prayed hard all the next day. That evening she called and said she had not gone through with it.

In Psalm 139, David praises God for overseeing his life, starting before he was born. David thanks God first for the fantastic way the human body is designed and constructed and then for the fact that every day of his life is "shaped" and "written down" by God (v. 16, NAB). If indeed God is the creator and designer of human life (and all other forms of life)—no one should treat that life lightly.

Marie C. Sanon
Saint John's University
Jamaica, New York

"I AM THE VINE, *you are the branches. Those who abide in me and I in them bear much fruit, because apart from me you can do nothing."*
(John 15:5)

Throughout the Bible, Jesus is referred to in a number of ways: as carpenter, teacher, fisherman, and shepherd. I cannot help but think of Jesus as a gardener as well.

It seems that in every teacher is a student; in every parent, a child; and in every artist, a piece of art. Jesus is both the bestower of life, the gardener—and life itself, the vine.

Certain traits characterize one who gardens: patience, faith, persistence, and especially an undying sense of optimism. Many artisans have been moved by the concept of the farmer, or sower. One such creator was the Dutch artist Vincent van Gogh. While other artists were depicting royalty, Van Gogh devoted his talents to portraying sowers and, in one work, potato eaters. His work is compelling, for it reflects them as faithful, productive, and dedicated. Jesus was a sower, spreading seeds wherever he went, stirring within us—life.

Coming from an Italian family, I learned to love and cherish the garden and its bounty. The garden, I believe, is a sacred place where hard work and honesty reign. All of us can be gardeners, and a garden can be anywhere at all, not just in one's own backyard. It can be on a windowsill, in the earth, or, in a surreal way, wherever you are. One's words and deeds can be the seeds of life.

To me Jesus epitomizes the roles of carpenter, teacher, fisherman, shepherd, and most of all, gardener—for his patience and love have nurtured within us what is necessary for life. How can we not grow and blossom with him taking care of us?

Karla Tramutola
Fairleigh Dickinson University
Teaneck, New Jersey

"CAN ANY OF YOU *by worrying add a single hour to your span of life? If then you are not able to do so small a thing as that, why do you worry about the rest? Consider the lilies, how they grow: they neither toil nor spin; yet I tell you, even Solomon in all his glory was not clothed like one of these.*"

(Luke 12:25–27)

On this rock I sit,
   many lifetimes of worries
   burden my young heart.
The wind whispers. The trees sway.
The birds sing . . . the Truth.
Suddenly, I grasp the simplistic power
   of leaving my troubles on this rock
   and letting the wind blow them away.
So my troubles whisper through the trees
   and sing to the birds
   and flow through the river of truth.
For the day He carried the cross,
   He made this rock,
   and with this rock my burdens
   are whisked away with nature's blessing.
So on this rock I stand and
   lift my hands to the sky,
   letting the Force flow through
   the world and me.
This is God's world, not mine.
My burdens are his.

Dawn Marie Weseli
University of Dayton
Dayton, Ohio

THOSE WHO ARE TAUGHT *the word*
must share in all good things with their teacher.
(Galatians 6:6)

People around me mumble and complain
about taking courses that are seemingly unnec-
essary and unrelated to their major. They fuss
and fight and seek justification for why they are
being forced to waste "their" money on classes
they don't want to take.

I know the complaint well, for I have lodged
the same one many times. But when all is said
and done, it just comes together. We may not
see the connections, but in God's eyes there are
no accidents. Everything God does is purposeful
and makes perfect sense to him. We ought to
strive to be more like God and to seek out the
goodness and righteousness in God's work. God
will show us meaning when we're ready to see
it.

God on high, let me be open to all that you'd
have me learn so that I can be effective in
helping others reach their goals. Amen.

Yolanda Dimitricia White
Alverno College
Milwaukee, Wisconsin

Then Jesus cried aloud: *"Whoever believes in me believes not in me but in him who sent me. And whoever sees me sees him who sent me. I have come as light into the world, so that everyone who believes in me should not remain in the darkness."*

(John 12:44–46)

We are beautiful;
the light of God's love shines from our eyes.
His grace is present in every step we take.
His blessings are evidenced in our smiles;
his suffering in our tears.
Not a word we speak is untouched
by his guidance.
The shining sun is his invitation to bask in its
glow and in his glory.
And the rainy day is not sadness,
but the chance to splash in puddles
and rediscover the simple joys of life.
The gentle breeze is his loving caress.
We are beautiful on the inside, always,
because God is smiling on us.
Revel in the knowledge that every day
is a present from God.
Celebrate life—joys and sorrows—
with enthusiasm.
God's hands are around us, over, under,
in front, and beside.
We will never fail, no matter how high
we climb.

Michelle Marie Colby
Virginia-Maryland Regional College of Veterinary Medicine
Blacksburg, Virginia

Index by School

Lycoming College
Williamsport, PA
Michelle Yvette Bissman 25

Marquette University
Milwaukee, WI
Sarah L. Buck 52

Messiah College
Grantham, PA
Martha Claire Truxton 26

Missouri Valley College
Marshall, MO
Margaret Tyler 115

Northwestern University
Evanston, IL
Krista Maren Puttler 121

Purdue University
West Lafayette, IN
Scott W. Hoffman 37

Rockford College
Rockford, IL
Clark L. Fabert Jr. 81

Rutgers University
New Brunswick, NJ
Justyna Braun 66

Saint Catharine College
Saint Catharine, KY
Elzie Burgher 33
Diana Kaye Chesser 86
Josh Newton 109
Julie Settles 131
Scott Spalding 90
Tricia 41

Saint John's University
Jamaica, NY
Kelly Anne Dobson 42
Marc Garcia 102
Michael R. Guerin 30, 79
Sonya Kim 70
Marie C. Sanon 137

Saint Joseph's College
Rensselaer, IN
Kimberly Anne Gabryel 94

Saint Mary's University of Minnesota
Winona, MN
Allison 50
Jill Arens 23
Eric Edward Aschenbrenner 77
Gretchen M. Baumgardt 29, 38
Lisa Marie Rose Brandt 16
C. C. 80
L. A. C. 95
Jennifer Elam 13
K. G. 39
Maranda Holt 59
Anthony C. Holter 89

Robert Horihan   110
Tracy Klassen   117
Jeffry Lusiak   104
Rebecca J. McAulay   72, 126
Karin McConville   36
B. D. Nelson   88
Jennifer Marie Novak   119
Daniel James Olsen   103
Susanne Quarfoth   127
Daniel Rech   134
Trisha Jean Reichenberger   107
Tait Schroeder   125
Joanne M. Tibble   46
Jennifer Tracy   120
Jessica J. Trom   57, 130

Saint Vincent College
Latrobe, PA
Will Ferguson   18

SUNY College at New Paltz
New Paltz, NY
Paul Wayne Benjamin   35

Towson University
Towson, MD
Stephanie T. Roberts   123, 132

University of Arizona
Tucson, AZ
Sheri Rugg   135

University of Cincinnati
Cincinnati, OH
Dennis A. Dziekan   101

University of Dayton
Dayton, OH
Brian C. Halderman   *54*
Robert C. Jones   *63*
Dawn Marie Weseli   *140*

University of Northern Iowa
Cedar Falls, IA
Luke Reisdorf   *51*

University of Northern Iowa
Fort Dodge, IA
Malinda Kesteloot   *22, 92*

University of Oklahoma
Norman, OK
Dave West   *129*

University of Scranton
Scranton, PA
Molly Buettner   *14, 21*
Christopher N. Steel   *43*

University of South Carolina
Columbia, SC
Megan Meece   *56, 65, 124*

University of Virginia
Charlottesville, VA
Sigrid R. Magid   *58, 122*

Virginia-Maryland Regional College of Veterinary Medicine
Blacksburg, VA
Michelle Marie Colby   *55, 142*

Viterbo College
La Crosse, WI
Kelly Benson   61
Jodi Lee Bodenberger   69
Jennifer Duckwitz   96
Jessica   112
Jennifer Kulzer   83
Christine Melko   12
Melissa J. Meyer   98
Andrea Kay Nelson   116
Jaimie D. Okusko   31
Christine Papke   73
Stephanie Anne Persick   91
Ann B. Schinderle   136
Krista Kathryn Webb   15
Meredith Dara Zondag   64

Wesleyan College
Macon, GA
Missy Graham   32 84

Weston Jesuit School of Theology
Cambridge, MA
Ann M. Michaud   108

West Texas A & M University
Canyon, TX
James C. Settles   105, 128

Acknowledgments (*continued*)

Notes, Reflections